THE ART OF MARBLED PAPER

THE ART OF
MARBLED PAPER

Marbled Patterns and How to Make Them

Einen Miura

Zaehnsdorf Ltd

London

First published 1988 by
Atelier Miura

English Language Edition
Published by Zaehnsdorf Ltd 1989
175R Bermondsey St, London SE1 3UW

Designed and produced by
Bellew Publishing Company Ltd
7 Southampton Place, London WC1A 2DR

Copyright © 1990 by Einen Miura

ISBN 0 947792 31 7

A limited edition of 150 signed copies, specially
bound by Zaehnsdorf, also available

ISBN 0 947792 40 6 limited edition

Printed and bound in Hong Kong by Regent Publishing
Services Ltd

CONTENTS

INTRODUCTION TO THE
ENGLISH LANGUAGE EDITION

When interest in marbling reached Japan, I realized that there was no literature available in Japanese. My passion for and interest in the subject led me to collect books on and about marbling to enable others in Japan to learn more about this fascinating art and its history. Finally, I wrote this book.

My wife and I, both separately and jointly, have been collecting marbled papers for 25 years and have many examples of both ancient and contemporary papers. However, we are proudest of our few thousand, full-sized, late 19th century examples.

We have ourselves been marbling for many years, including the production of 6000 sheets for the 'Elephant Folio' facsimile edition of Audubon's *Birds of America*. It was necessary to make a giant-sized trough to produce the papers, and the project itself took a year to complete. This was a particularly great challenge for my wife as she had to experiment with various techniques in order to create an appropriate image for both the content of the book and its contemporary production. The technique which she invented for this project she called 'oleaugraphy', a combination of three words and three languages: 'o' – oil; 'l'eau' – water; 'graphy' – writing.

My primary aim in writing this book was to describe the equipment necessary for setting up a workshop and the materials required for production, and to introduce and explain various marbling techniques. I have tried to do the latter by means of clear diagrams showing the sequence of operations necessary for the production of certain patterns.

I have dated patterns where possible, but this has proved difficult as patterns reached different countries at different dates and the available literature is very contradictory. I have given pattern titles in three different languages so that they might be more readily recognized in the relevant countries.

Some of the reproductions in this book show patterns that we have created, while others are known to us only from the one example that we possess. I have taken the liberty of naming the latter so that there might be less confusion in the future.

I would like to thank my publisher for giving me the opportunity to share the beauty of our collection with other lovers of marbled paper, and hope that this book will excite and give pleasure, stirring in each of you a creativity which I believe all possess.

THE HISTORY AND DEVELOPMENT OF MARBLED PAPER

The Origin of Marbled Paper

N the 16th century, a new way of decorating paper was introduced to Europe from the Middle and Far East – designs that resembled the veins in marble. This effect was created by throwing or dripping inks on to a size (a mucilaginous solution), where they were allowed to float freely or were sculpted into patterns. A sheet of paper was carefully placed on to the surface of the size and the design lifted off.

The general term for this process is *marbling*. It is similar to the technique known as *suminagashi* ('ink floating') in Japan, which has been handed down as a major art form since ancient times, when the pale grey swirls of ink served as a decorative background for the calligraphy of the nobility. *Suminagashi* is produced by floating ink on water, to which pine tree oil or turpentine has been added as a dispersant. Traditionally only black ink stones were used, which limited the colour range to various shades of grey; centuries later, red and blue were added to the repertoire. Today 'sumi sets' are commercially available which contain many colours, all of which produce good results.

By touching the surface of the water very lightly, first with the brush containing the ink and then the brush containing the oil, and repeating this procedure a number of times, a series of very controlled concentric circles – a traditional design – is produced. This is lifted from the surface of the water in the same manner as used for marbled paper.

In marbling, the pigments of the inks are heavier than those used in *suminagashi*, and will not float unaided. A size is therefore necessary. The colours already contain a dispersant (ox gall) which helps them to spread over the surface of the size. The amount of dispersant is determined by the order in which the colours are to be used in the pattern – less for the first, most for the last.

Brushes do not touch the surface in marbling. The inks are thrown or dripped on to the size where they are allowed to float freely or are manoeuvred into patterns. The patterns are transferred to paper (which has been treated with alum) by carefully resting it on the surface of the size for a few seconds. When the paper is lifted off, the design is fixed to the paper.

To my knowledge, marbling was carried out as early as the 15th century in China, India, Persia and Turkey where it became an integral part of pictures rather than a background decoration. Marbling has been used in a variety of ways: as a background for calligraphy; as borders on picture frames; and as a base for silhouettes. This latter application of marbling can be found in a small Persian painting, *The Princes of the Hunt*, created during the reign of Shah Tahmasp (1524–70), and in miniatures held by the Islamic Department of the Metropolitan Museum of Art in New York. More of this mixing of techniques can be found in the Turkish and Persian miniatures; the *Cheval étique* from the late 16th century, now owned by the Asiatic Studies Department of the Boston Museum of Fine Arts, and in the Turkish miniature of *c.* 1150, *The Cow Nursing Calf* in the Fogg Museum of Art at Harvard University. Other miniatures showing similar marbling methods can be found in the Bibliothèque Nationale in Paris and in the British Library in London. In the Freer Gallery of the Smithsonian Institution in Washington D.C. is a beautiful, delicately executed, combed marble frame surrounding a *Virgin and Child*, which was painted in India around 1625.

In the book *Miniature Painting and Painters of Persia, India and Turkey from the 8th to the 18th century*, published in London in 1912, F. R. Martin describes marbled pictures created around the year 1500, including paintings of animals and a man on a horse. Some of the animals were given shape through marbling, while others were drawn with a pen. It is remarkable that decorative papers requiring such advanced technology could be produced so many centuries ago.

Another source that attests to the fact that these decorative papers were produced long ago in India and Persia is the book *Survey of Persian Art*, published in 1939 in Britain under the sponsorship of the American Institute for Iranian Art and Archaeology. In a chapter entitled 'Marbelized or *Abri* Paper',* H. Taherzade Behzad states that, in Persia during the first part of the 15th century, marbling art was used for flyleaves in books, as a background on paper used for calligraphy, or simply as borders of pages. He also states that the Persians of that time knew five ways of marbling – simple *abri*, combed *abri*, flowery *abri*, linear *abri* and gilded *abri* – evidence of the Persians' remarkable diversity in this art.

Sir Thomas Herbert, an English diplomat who travelled in Persia, described marbled paper in his book *Travels in Persia 1627–1629*. He says that 'their paper is very glossy and, by dropping oiled colours, chamleted and veined like marble.'

When marbling was introduced into Europe, it served the same functions as it had in the East. It formed the backdrops to coats-of-arms, family trees and the like. It also, until recent times, had a more practical use: the edges of account books were marbled, and if any papers were removed from these

---

*Marbling is called '*abri*' in Persian. The literal meaning is 'cast Shadow' but in this case it is more likely to mean 'varied'.

ledgers, this would interrupt the flow of the delicate design and show up immediately.

Because early marbled paper served as a background decoration, the inks were pale so that the pattern did not disturb the image of the text. It was not until approximately 100 years after its introduction that marbled paper with a more colourful design was produced, to be used as the linings of boxes and as the endpapers of bookbindings.

With the passage of time, marbling became increasingly popular and many patterns were created. However, the technique was practised by only a few, and marbling was regarded as a 'secret art'. By the late 19th century, the process had become so well known that marbled paper could be mass produced and, as a result, people finally began to tire of it. Although marbling experienced a brief resurgence when the Viennese artists of the Art Deco school created hauntingly beautiful images, demand for marbling slowed down. Then suddenly interest reawakened in the late 1950s, and now marbling is enormously popular again.

Marbled paper in old documents

THE oldest documents in which *suminagashi* is mentioned are in the *waka* (traditional Japanese poems) of Ariwara no Shigeharu in *Kokin Waka Shu*. Shigeharu (whose dates of birth and death are unknown) was the son of Narihira (825–80), a famous Japanese poet, which means that *suminagashi* must have been in use by the end of the 9th century.

The earliest known extant example of *suminagashi* can be found in *Sanju-roku nin Kashu*, a collection of the selected works of 36 eminent poets published in about AD 1112. It is said that marbled paper was produced in China from 1369 to 1644 using a technique similar to *suminagashi*, but this theory has not been substantiated. It is possible, however, that the technology for the production of *suminagashi* travelled from Japan to China and Turkey via the Silk Road across Asia.

Professor Mehmed Ali Kagitci, in his article 'Ebru, or Turkish Marbled Papers' in *Pallete* (no. 30, 1968, Basle, Switzerland), states that there are 12 patterns in Turkish marbled paper (in Turkish, marbling is called 'ebru', which means 'clouds'):

1 *Akkase-ebru* ('white spot marble') is only faintly coloured, or does not appear at all underneath the written or illuminated part of the paper, but only in those areas surrounding the writing or picture.

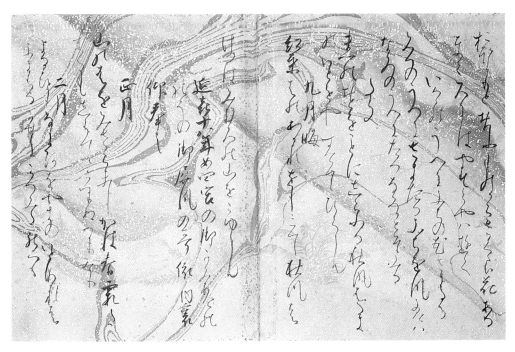

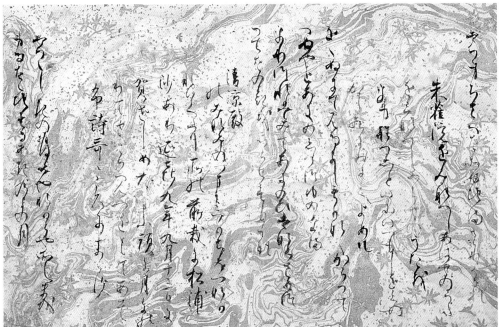

Sanjuroku nin Kashu of the Nishihonganji Temple, a national treasure of Japan.

This oldest and most perfect collection of the selected works of 36 eminent poets was bound in *c.* AD 1112. The paper was decorated using various techniques, including cutting and pasting, the affixing of gold and silver leaf, and *suminagashi*. The traditional Japanese poems known as *waka* were written on these pages in a flowing style. The beauty of this work is incomparable, and it is the oldest example of *suminagashi* in existence.

The examples shown here are the *waka* in *Tsurayuki Shu* (above) and *Mitsune Shu* (below). Each is roughly 200 by 300 mm.

2 *Ebrulu-akkase* ('coloured spot marble'). The part of the paper on which writing appears is always faintly marbled with light colours.

3 *Battal-ebru* (*battal*='large') has a marble pattern with prominent veins.

4 *Somaki-ebru* (*somaki*='coloured') is a traditional coloured marbled paper.

5 *Hafif-ebru* (*hafif*='weak/pale'). A very faintly coloured marbled paper used for official documents and calligraphy.

6 *Kumlu-ebru* (*kumlu*='sandy') is likewise modest in appearance, with a fine-grained pattern containing little or no embellishment.

7 *Hatip-ebrusu* ('preacher marble') is a pattern of flowers and leaves comprising carnations, roses and tulips.

8 *Necmeddin-ebrescu* ('flower marble') shows coloured flowers, together with stems and leaves, upon a monochrome marbled ground.

9 *Trakli-ebru* ('comb marble') is of conventional character, with a marbled pattern produced by a comb.

10 *Tarama-* or *gitgel-ebru* (*tarama*='hatching'; *gitgel*='zigzag') has an irregular zigzag hatched pattern.

11 *Tarzikadim battal-ebru* (*tarzikadim*='antique style') is an attractive stone marbled pattern.

12 *Yazili-ebru* (*yazili*='written, decorated with calligraphy') is a marbled paper in which the area devoted to calligraphy is blocked out and therefore appears white on the coloured sheet.

Several books that contain original marbled paper from various periods in Turkey still exist today. One, held by the Stuttgart Library in West Germany, was found by Georg Ringler of Strasburg when he travelled to Constantinople in 1581. It contains 63 sheets decorated on both sides and three sheets embellished on one side only. All of them display the stone marbled paper known as 'Turkish battal' and incorporate pale shades of blue, yellow, red, green, brown and grey.

In western Europe, the makers of the *album amicorum* made use of a marbling technique similar to Turkish battal. An *album amicorum* was a friendship book popular in Europe during the 16th and 17th centuries. It contained decorative papers, sometimes interleaved with marbled papers, and was carried by travellers. The Victoria & Albert Museum in London has an example of such a book, which was carried by Wolfgang Leutkauff, a Viennese who travelled to Constantinople, Adrianople and Belgrade between the years 1616 and 1632. It consists of 288 pages and displays 34 types of marble on 46 sheets. Similar examples are held by the British Museum (one of which contains 24 original marbled papers) and by the Bodleian Library of Oxford University. These excellent examples of marbled paper well substantiate the fact that marbling was being created in Turkey in the 17th century.

Turkish marbling was also discussed in two other notable and reliable sources. In his *A relation of a Journey begun Ani Domi 1610: Foure Bookes containing a description of the Turkish Empire of Aegypt, of the Holy Land, of the Remote parts of Italy and the Islands adjoining* (1615), the English author and traveller George Sandys said: 'The Turks curiously sleeke their paper which is thicke much of it being coloured and dappled like chamolets done by a tricke they have dipping it in water.' And Sir Francis Bacon, the noted Renaissance philosopher and statesman, wrote, in his book *Sylva Sylvarum*, published in 1627:

> The Turks have a pretty art of chamoletting of paper which is not with us in use. They take divers oyled colours and put them severally (in drops) upon water; and stir the water lightly; and then wet their paper (being of some thickness) with it; and the paper will be waved and veined like chamolet, or marble.

In *The History of Printing and Books*, published in 1689 in Paris, Jean La Caille states that Macé Ruette, a stationer and bookbinder, invented the marbling art and used it for 'end sheets'. This statement must be erroneous since marbling can be seen in Turkish miniatures of the very early 17th century.

The marbled paper that reached Europe in the 16th century was mainly used by binders. Le Gascon of France incorporated marbled paper in his bindings between 1617 and 1630. An example of those he used is to be found in the book *Noramu Testament Grase* which was published in Amsterdam in 1633 and can be seen today in the British Library. Florimund Badier of France was also active in bookbinding, around 1650, and used marbled paper for both flyleaves and covers on some of his books. Marbled papers made with red, blue and yellow inks can be found as endpapers of his *Le Tableau de la Croix presente dans les Ceremonies de la Ste Messe* and his *Explication familiere et morale par Francis Pean*, which were both published in 1651 in Paris.

The colours used for Turkish marble before and during this period were mostly pale but very beautiful, and were based on red, blue and yellow. They show both stone and combed patterns. The book *Traité historique et pratique de la gravure en bois*, written by J. M. Papillon and published in Paris in 1766, states that, in the 17th century, the Le Bretons, father and son, had freely applied more complicated techniques to produce beautiful marbled paper with gold veins.

From the Far East and Middle East to Europe

OW did the art of marbling travel from the Middle East and Far East to Europe? Trading and cultural exchange between East and West developed more and more, thus increasing awareness of different cultures. It is generally accepted that, during this age, the technology of marbling was first brought to Europe by Venetian merchants, who acted as a bridge between Orient and Occident. During the 16th and 17th centuries, marbling was introduced into Italy, and then to France, Germany, Spain, Holland, Britain and other countries in northern Europe, both by land and sea routes. The larger European cities, which were international trading centres, saw many new exciting things change hands. Therefore all kinds of exotic goods – including marbled paper – reached far-away places.

Daniel Schwenter, a mathematician and scholar of Oriental languages who died in 1636, appears to have been the first person to write about marbling technology in Europe. In his book *In Deliciae Physico-Mathematicae* [or *der Mathemet*] *und philosophische Erquickstunden*, published in Nuremburg in 1651–53, there is a chapter entitled 'Turkisches Papyr zu machen und zu figuriren' ('How to make and decorate Turkish papers'), in which he describes the making of flower designs:

> When I wish to make figures on paper, as for example a rose, I throw on the solution a drop of colour-red, yellow or blue. On this drop of colour on the solution I let fall several drops of alcohol (*Spiritus Vini*) which pushes the red, yellow or blue colour out from the other in the circles. In this space I throw again another drop of the aforesaid colour, and again the alcohol as often as I want until the flower or rose is the size desired. Then I form the leaves and the rest with a quill or a pointed fine stick.

(This description was included in the pamphlet *Some Notes on the Art of Marbling Paper in the Seventeenth Century* by Charles M. Adams, published in New York in 1947.)

As Europe entered the 17th century, interest in marbled paper developed gradually, and a few books of research were published. In 1646, Athanasius Kircher, a priest, mathematician and Oriental linguist, published the book *Ars magna lucis et umbra* in Rome. This includes sections on how to make Turkish marble, how to make inks from natural materials and how to make marbled paper with a feathered pattern. Many researchers who study decorative papers and wall papers today claim that Kircher's book was the first to introduce the art of marbled paper in Europe.

Several years later, Casper Schott, Kircher's most trusted student, wrote about Kircher and his marbled papers. He described Kircher as an artist who worked very hard: 'He made whole figures of men, of animals, trees, cities and regions on paper . . . now by a design as profuse as waves of the sea, now in a variety of marble, sometimes in the many colours of the plumes of birds and many other designs.' In Schott's eyes, this was 'an invention completely marvellous and full of mysteries'.

Schott also published a book in Latin, *Magia universalis naturae et artis, sive recondita naturalium et artificalium rerum scientia*, which was published in Wurzburg in 1657 and contained a chapter entitled 'Chartum variis coloribus more Turcico pingere' or 'How to make Turkish marbled paper designs using various inks'.

In 1662, two years after the Restoration, when Charles II reclaimed the throne of England, the Englishman John Evelyn, who had met and known Kircher almost 20 years earlier, gave a lecture at the Royal Society concerning the making of marbled paper, covering marbling, size, inks, technique and paper. The manuscript used by Evelyn for that lecture is currently part of the Sir Hans Sloane Collection maintained by the British Museum in London. In a diary entry dated 8 November 1644, Evelyn describes the day he visited Kircher at the Jesuit Church in Rome while travelling in Italy.

Father Kircher showed us many singular courtesies, leading us into their refectory, dispensatory, laboratory . . . and finally into his own study, where, with Dutch patience, he showed us his perpetual motions . . . and a thousand other crotchets and devices. . .

Although Evelyn's lecture was given in 1662, it was not made public until 37 years later, when in 1699 John Houghton published it in his weekly folio, *Husbandry and Trade Improv'd*. During the interim, the only known record of marbling in England was a short item written by Robert Boyle, the father of modern chemistry, in 1670.

In Germany, however, Johann Kunckel von Lowenstjern published a two-volume work, *Ars vitraria experimentalis*, in 1679 in Frankfurt and Leipzig, in which he gave a detailed description of marbling techniques. This remains an important source of information concerning marbling in Europe. In addition, Antonio Meri published *De alti vitraria* which also describes how marbled papers are made.

A 18th-century marbling studio: Taken from *Encyclopédie ou dictionnaire raisonné des sciences, des arts et des métiers*, edited by Denis Diderot and Jean le Rond d'Alembert (35 volumes, issued 1751–80, Paris).

From left to right
- Grinding pigment to make ink.
- Transferring on to paper a pattern made by dripping ink on to size.
- Dripping ink on to size.
- Using a comb to make a pattern.
- Hanging marbled paper on a line for drying.
- Making marbling size.

The development of marbling in Europe (17th–18th centuries)

B Y the 17th century, marbling techniques had been developed in France, Germany and Holland, and beautiful marbled papers were starting to be produced. In the 18th century, those techniques were actively exported to many other countries.

In the first chapter of his book *The Art of Bookbinding*, published in

A 18th-century marbling studio: Taken from *Encyclopédie ou dictionnaire raisonné des sciences, des arts et des métiers*, edited by Denis Diderot and Jean le Rond d'Alembert (35 volumes, issued 1751–80, Paris).

From left to right
- Marbling the edges of books.
- Making a pattern with a stylus.
- Folding paper.
- Polishing marbled paper using a stone attached to the tip of a shaft fixed to the ceiling.
- Polishing marbled paper

London in 1880, Joseph W. Zaehnsdorf notes that Dutch marbled papers in foolscap size (*c.* 30 × 40 cm) were often exported to England as wrapping paper for toys. Since customs duties were levied on goods imported into England at that time, many exporters wrapped toys and other small objects in marbled paper before sending them there, to escape paying duty on the papers. The marbled papers were later carefully removed from the toys and smoothed out and sold to bookbinders who used them as decoration for book covers, as endpapers, for boxes and so on. This claim is substantiated by Charles W. Woolnough in his book *The Whole Art of Marbling* (London,

1881) and by Rosamond B. Loring in her *Decorated Book Papers* (Cambridge, Massachusetts, 1942).

From the latter part of the 17th century to the middle of the 18th century, marbled papers were also produced in England, but their colour, pattern, quality and other attributes were not as good as those imported from Germany and Holland, and they were therefore not very popular. This situation was in part rectified in the middle of the 18th century when the Society for the Encouragement of Arts, Manufactures and Commerce decided to award prizes for excellence in marbled paper production. It offered £50 to anyone who could make 40 reams of paper (1 ream = 480 sheets) that were of the same quality as imported marbled papers, and £25 to anyone making 20 reams.

This provided a strong financial incentive as the prizes represented a large amount of money. In 1763, two marbled paper craftsmen were selected to receive the awards – Henry Houseman received the £50 prize, and Samuel Harvey the £25. By these means, the quality of marbled paper in England slowly improved. Several marblers began to publicize their papers, notably Richard Dymott, who advertised his own French and Dutch marbles, and William Weber, who produced papers in *c.* 1770. In 1788, the Society of Arts awarded a medal to John Davis, a bookbinder, in recognition of the beauty of his books, which were bound using his own handmade marbled papers. It is said that his work continued until 1802.

Special Circumstances surrounding marbling

THE method of production of marbled paper was kept a closely guarded secret for many years, being regarded as a special skill which should not be taught to those outside the trade. There are, therefore, not very many reference books from which to learn about early techniques. The method of manufacture is really not very difficult, but details were never shared with the public. The craftsmen who produced the papers were afraid that their livelihoods would be jeopardized should the methods of production become widely known. Although outstanding marbles were produced, the secrecy surrounding their manufacture had an unfortunate backlash, as untimely deaths meant that the methods for producing certain kinds of paper were not passed on to successors, and therefore the secrets of how to make the papers died with their keepers.

This situation of particular methods of production being handed down in secret was not confined to earlier centuries or simply to book manufacture. It was general practice in almost every field of production and continues even to this day. Bookbinding is, however, an especially good illustration – for example, the gold tooling of books was for many years a skill which was only taught to a select handful of craftsmen. This practice has the effect of stunting the advancement and growth of a craft and of restricting the spread of knowledge and hence the future continuation of the skills. It has already contributed greatly to the decline of the hand-crafted bookbinding industry as a commercially viable concern.

An example of this is illustrated by the book *Bibliopegia, or the Art of Bookbinding in All its Branches*, which was published in 1835 in London. This is said to be the first book to introduce and describe the decoration of leather bindings, and was written by John Hannett using the pseudonym John Andrews Arnett. Hannett was forced to use a pen name as it was the only way that he could openly present this information without being ostracized within his trade. He was also attempting to extend an opportunity for professions to exchange information while remaining within the traditional boundaries of his own trade. In his book, Hannett devoted 19 pages to various marbling techniques.

The development of marbling in modern times

ROM the latter part of the 17th century through the 18th century, a variety of marbled papers were produced in France and Germany, most of them being made in small studios. The papers were of excellent quality, and there was a large demand for them.

In the book *Nouveau manuel complet de fabricant de papiers de fantaisie* ('Complete New Guide for Decorative Paper Production') by M. Fichtenberg, which was published in 1852 in Paris, there are descriptions of marbled papers and other decorative papers produced by Alois Dessaur and others in factories and studios in various parts of Germany such as Prussia, Saxony and Offenbach. A total of 32 original samples of marbled paper are included in this book.

Technological advances made it possible for marbled paper to be produced by machines, with a resulting change in the appearance of the papers. By the middle of the 19th century, the surface of marbled paper could be glazed by running it through heated metal cylinders; this had previously been accomplished by coating it with beeswax and by polishing it with a stone.

In the late 19th century, Josef Halfer, a bookbinder in Budapest, made a tremendous impact on marbling. He created unique techiques that combined new materials with traditional skills, and blended several excellent methods into a single, more integrated one. He considered it his duty to pass on his findings to the next generation, and for me, his book – *Die Fortschritte der Marmorierkunst*, first published in Budapest in 1885 – is still the most important source of information on marbling techniques. Halfer's expertise and understanding of the subject helped many people, not just a few crafts-men, and furthermore, he was instrumental in simplifying the craft and making materials easier to work with.

Until Halfer's time, marbled paper had been produced using a vegetable size called 'gum arabic' or 'gum tragacanth' which enabled the inks to float on the surface. In his book, Halfer introduced a size produced from a seaweed base, carragheen moss, a technique that is today in general use throughout the world. It was universally adopted because it lasts much longer than gum, and allows for the finest combing techniques to be used with ease. He also produced better inks for use in conjunction with this new size.

The original book consisted of 224 pages of description and 35 samples of original marbled paper. A second edition was published in Stuttgart in 1891, with a French version published in Geneva in 1894. In the same year, an English translation by Herman Dieck was published under the title *The Progress of the Marbling Art from Technical Scientific Principles* in Buffalo, New York. When this was published in London 1904, it was renamed *The Art of Marbling and the Treatment of the New Bronze Colours: A Practical Guide to Marbling by Halfer's Method*.

Following publication of Halfer's book, marbling was taught around the world in schools, paper factories and bookbinderies, and a number of other books on the subject followed in quick succession. The most popular of these were:

- *The Mysterious Marbler* by James Sumner, originally published in London in 1854; reprinted with a new introduction in 1976.

- *Die Marmorierskunst* by Joseph Hauptmann, published in German in 1895, 2nd edition 1901, 3rd edition 1906.

- *Das Marmorieren des Buchbinders auf Schleimgrund und im Kleisterver-fahren* . . . ('Process of Marbling Art Using Seaweed and Paste') by Paul Adam, published in German in 1906, 2nd edition 1923.

- *Die Marmorierkunst* ('The Art of Marbling') by Paul Kersten, published in German in 1922, and in Norwegian in 1925.

- *Die Kunst des Marmorierens* ('The Marblers' Art') by Franz Weisse, published in German in 1940, and in English in 1980.
- *Buntpapier: Herkommen, Geschichte, Techniken, Beziehungen zur Kunst* by Albert Haemmerle, published in 1961.
- *Marbling: A History and a Bibliography* by Phoebe J. Easton, published in 1983 in Los Angeles.
- *Le Papier marbré son Histoire et sa Fabrication* ('Marble Paper: Its History and Production') by Marie-Ange Doizy and Stephane Ipert, published in 1985 in Paris.

There is currently much research being done into the history and techniques of marbling, which will hopefully open up the field considerably and increase general information in the near future.

HOW TO PRODUCE MARBLED PAPERS

Inks react to the slightest differences in water – temperature, pH (degree of acidity or alkalinity), hardness – and to the humidity of the surrounding air. It is not therefore possible to give exact recipes for the preparation of inks that will give perfect results every time. Quantities are mentioned within the text, but will have to be experimented with in order to produce perfect results under your own conditions.

Equipment

Clothing

Marbling is a messy business, and the wearing of overalls is advisable as anything one wears for marbling is likely to become ink stained.

Rubber gloves

These are also advisable, to prevent one's hands becoming impregnated with pigment.

(1)

Towels

Several damp towels should be kept to hand in order to keep the equipment and work surface clean.

Pot (*illustration no. 1*)

A cooking pot with a capacity of 20–30 litres is used to boil the carragheen moss used to form the marbling size.

Metal sieve (*illustration no. 2*)

This is necessary to remove the boiled seaweed fibre from the size.

(2)

Muslin

Soft muslin is used to strain the sieved carragheen size.

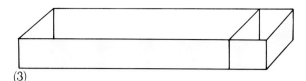

(3)

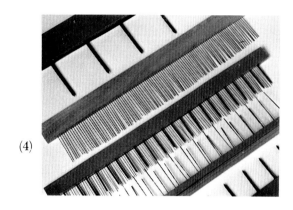

(4)

(5)

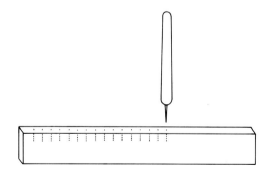

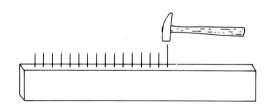

Marbling trough *(illustration no. 3)*

This can be made of plastic, wood or stainless steel and is used to hold the carragheen size. Photographic developing trays make good troughs as they usually consist of two parts; excess size can be caught in the smaller section as the marbled sheet is pulled over the dividing rim between the two portions while being removed. Ideally, the marbling trough should be 10–20 cm larger than the size of paper that one is likely to use.

Combs *(illustration no. 4)*

These are easy to make if not commercially available. There are many different types, producing various effects, and several different ways to make them. The following three methods are the easiest.

1 *(illustration no. 5)* Take a wooden board 15–20 mm thick and cut to fit the width or length of the trough. Mark off the positions of the teeth with a ruler to ensure accuracy, and, using an awl, make small holes at these marks. Finally, carefully tap the teeth – which can be pre-cut piano (steel) wire, long straight pins or nails – into the holes with a hammer. Ideally, the teeth should protrude by about 3–7 cms.

2 *(illustration no. 6)* Using two boards cut to the length or width of the trough, carefully mark the positions of the teeth and score shallow grooves in the wood.

Balsa wood is ideal for making these boards as scoring is much easier. Finally the teeth are put into position and the two boards bonded together with adhesive.

3 *(illustration no. 7)* The same method employed for board no. 1 above is used to create a comb which has two rows of teeth spaced at 20–30 mm intervals. This double-toothed comb is necessary to create such marbles as peacock marble *(see* p. 117) and bouquet marble (p. 118).

(6)

Thick paper and pressing boards
Before use, the stack of alum-treated paper lies sandwiched between thick absorbent paper and pressing boards.

Weights
Weights are placed on to the alum-treated paper so that some of its dampness will be retained. Paper should ideally be treated the night before it is to be marbled.

(7)

Thermometer, hygrometer, water thermometer *(illustration nos. 8–9)*
The room temperature, room humidity and size temperature should be taken during marbling and a detailed record maintained. This will allow marbling to be precise and will ensure that you will be able to reproduce patterns accurately in the future.

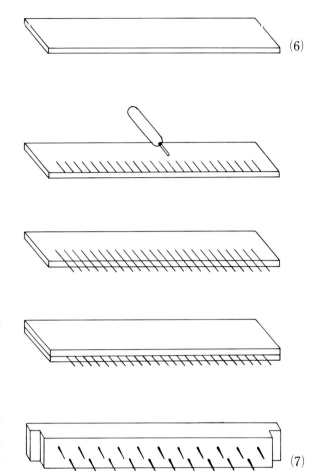

(8)

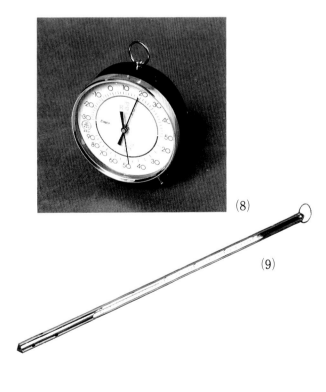

(9)

(10)

Sponge

This is used to treat the paper with alum before marbling can take place. The sponge can be natural or man-made.

Scales *(illustration no. 10)*

Scales with a capacity of up to 2 kg are used to weigh such things as the carragheen moss, alum and borax.

(11)

Drop bottles *(illustration nos. 11–14)*

These are made of either glass or plastic, and allow for the addition of exact quantities of ink.

Measuring cup *(illustration no. 15)*

A cup graduated up to 100 cc in 5 cc increments is most useful for measuring

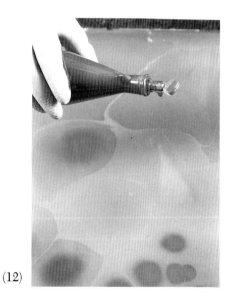

(12)

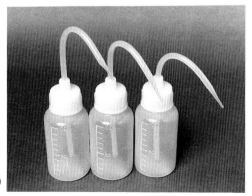

(13)

the amount of water for the alum solution, and for diluting inks.

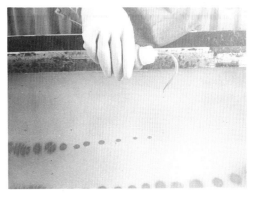

(14)

Funnel (*illustration no. 16*)
Funnels are used to put inks into the drop bottles and for returning unused inks to their storage containers (*illustration no. 17*).

(15)

Stylus (*illustration no. 18*)
This can take many forms, but is generally made from a needle, a piece of piano wire or a sliver of bamboo, affixed to a cork for easy handling. An awl could also be used (*illustration no. 19*). The stylus is employed to move the marble colours into their desired patterns on the size.

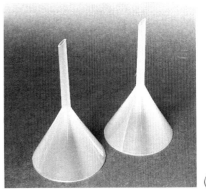

(16)

(17)

33

(18)

(19)

(20)

(21)

Rinsing board

After the papers have been marbled, they are placed on to a board and the carragheen solution is washed off. The board should ideally be longer and wider than the paper, and can be made of wood, glass or stainless steel. Washing marbled paper without the support of a board results in the paper creasing and tearing as well as inadequate rinsing.

Marbling brushes *(illustration nos. 20–23)*
These are made from a bristle broom *(no. 20)*, which is taken apart. The bristles are grouped together in small bunches, cut to various lengths to form brushes of different sizes and then rebound *(no. 22)*.

(22)

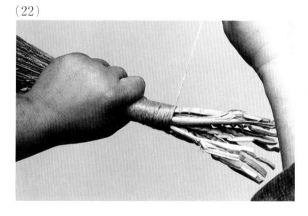

(23)

Drop brushes *(illustration no. 24–26)*
Drop brushes are very useful for controlling the pace at which drops are applied to the size as they hold quite a large amount of ink. Calligraphy, oil or water colour brushes can also be used.

Ink storage jars *(illustration no. 27)*
Glass jars are ideal for storing inks as it is easy to see the colours. Jars should have screw or snap-top lids as this allows inks to be kept for quite some time. They should also have necks about 6–8 cm wide to allow use with drop brushes.

Bowls and cups *(illustration nos. 28–29)*
These can be used with marbling brushes and can be made of stainless steel, glass, ceramic or plastic.

(26)

(27)

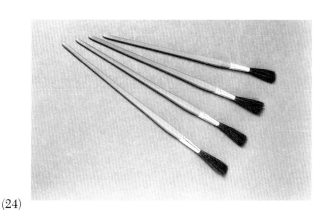

(24)

(28)

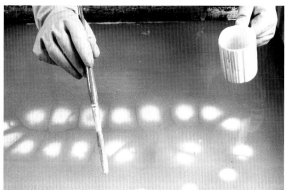

(25)

(29)

35

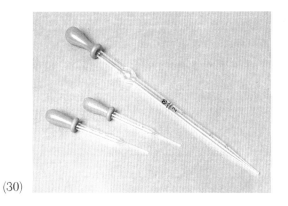
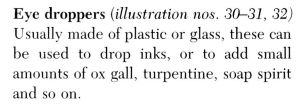

(30)

Eye droppers (*illustration nos. 30–31, 32*)
Usually made of plastic or glass, these can be used to drop inks, or to add small amounts of ox gall, turpentine, soap spirit and so on.

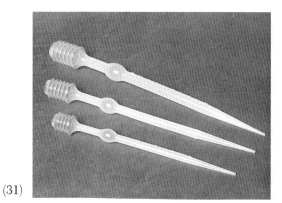

(31)

Assistance rod
Ink drops of equal size and quantity can be produced by holding a rod in one hand and an ink-soaked brush in the other. When the brush is moved forwards in a throwing motion, the rod stops the movement. With each contact, equal amounts of ink are sprinkled over the trough. Move the rod vertically upwards until the whole surface of the size is covered. If just a few sheets of paper are being marbled, a forearm can be used to stop the throwing motion.

(32)

Cleaning paper *(illustration no. 33)*
These pieces of paper should be roughly 5–8 cm wide and the width of the trough. They are used to 'scrape' the surface of the size after each sheet of marble is completed, to clean it before inks are re-applied.

(33)

Drying rack *(illustration no. 34)*
As in lithographic, silk screen or wood block printing, marbled paper is placed right side up for drying. Racks vary according to preference and individual conditions. The one illustrated here is made of metal and has 50 shelves that are 100 mm on their longest side. If drying racks like these are not available, then the marbled paper can be hung over a line to dry. Circulation of the air is the most important factor here.

(34)

Materials

Carragheen moss

This is a seaweed found off the coast of Iceland and Ireland – hence its alternate name 'Irish moss'. It can be bought either in dried, or powdered form. The former is boiled to provide a size on which the inks will float freely. This seaweed provides a particularly good medium as it has a mucous quality which sustains the inks well.

Borax

Marbling requires water that does not contain too many mineral salts, and borax is used to soften water which is too hard. As water differs everywhere, it will be necessary to experiment with the water you are using and to adjust the amount of borax according to requirements.

Paper

Most papers that are commercially available can be used for marbling, with the exception of high gloss/art papers, as contact with water dissolves their surface. The paper should be cut to just less than the size of the trough, and should, in most cases, be treated with alum prior to marbling.

Inks

Until fairly recently, preparing inks for marbling was a complex procedure, with pigments having to be ground and water and alcohol added proportionally to make the inks react correctly. These days, however, one can take advantage of the ready-made inks that are available. Water-soluble acrylic paints and water colours can also be used when thinned with water to the correct density. Oil based inks are used with petrol to control its spreading.

Ox gall

This transparent, slightly yellowish liquid is added to the inks to control the speed at which they spread when dropped on to the size. It is not used for watercolour, acrylic or oil-based inks.

Alum

This colourless, transparent acid in octahedral-crystal form is used to treat paper prior to marbling. It is widely employed in mordants, medicines and the manufacture of paper. The solution is made by mixing 50–80 grams of alum with 1 litre of water.

(35)

Preparing to marble

Preparation of the workroom

To produce the best results, the workroom must meet certain conditions. First, it must not be subject to direct sunlight, or to fluctuating environmental conditions such as rapid changes in temperature or humidity. Second, it must be large enough to provide adequate space for marbling and for drying the marble paper. Third, the room must have a permanent water supply and drainage system so that a lot of water can be used without difficulty.

For smooth and speedy processing, all tools and materials must be arranged close to hand. It is also a good idea to put plastic sheeting on the floor, and to cover this with newspaper, as water and inks can occasionally be sprayed around the workshop quite liberally. Keep a large supply of newspaper handy so that these floor papers can be changed often. Illustration no. 36 shows an example of a marbler's studio.

(36)

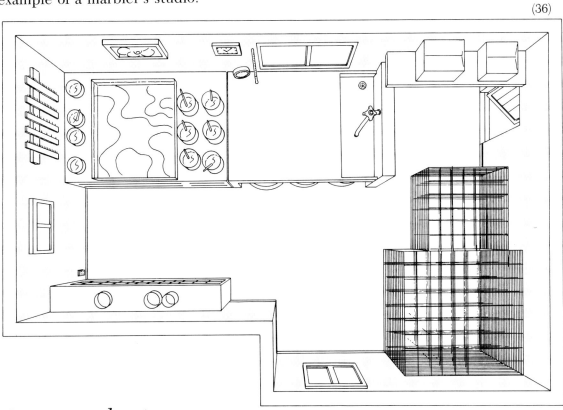

Preparing the size

Perhaps the most important aspect of marbling is preparing an adequate size.

A standard recipe is 15 g carragheen moss per litre of water, and 15 g borax per 6 litres of water (although this last measure may vary according to the hardness of the water you use). The desired quantity of the above mixture is put into a large pot (*illustration no. 37*) and slowly brought to the boil while being stirred constantly. The mixture is then removed from the heat and half a litre of cold water is added for every 15 litres of mixture. It is then stirred well and allowed to cool for 12–24 hours. At the end of this time, the residue moss fibres are strained from the mixture and the remaining size is then ladled on to muslin stretched over a large bucket (*no. 38*) and strained through. This removes any dirt, dust and other small impurities, leaving only pure, clean size.

Obtaining the correct density of size can be a delicate matter. If it is too thick, the colours will not move and spread on the surface but sink. Alternatively, if the size is too thin, the inks will simply spread far too quickly to

(37)　　(38)

allow for the creation of any designs. The proper size should have the consistency of cream. The density can be adjusted by the addition of more water if it is too thick, or by more moss solution if it is too thin. Be sure to allow the size to stand between each alteration.

The size should always be poured into the marbling trough the evening before it is intended to be used, to allow dispersal of any air bubbles which would disturb the design. Whenever the size is not being used, it should be covered to prevent the surface from becoming full of impurities such as dust.

At the beginning of a marbling session, it may be found that the surface of the size has developed a jelly-like quality due to contact with the air. This is easily removed by scraping it off with the cleaning paper described earlier.

The temperature of the size is of great importance, as the higher the temperature, the quicker the inks will spread over the surface, making control of the design much more difficult. At too low a temperature, the size will start to thicken, which will make the designs irregular. The ideal temperature for marbling is 20–22°C, and not lower than 18°C.

Making and using alum solution

Alum solution is made by adding 50–80 grams of alum to 1 litre of water and heating slowly until it is all dissolved. Prior to marbling, a sponge is used to apply this solution to the side of the paper which will receive the marble (*illustration no. 39*). This is done to ensure that the ink adheres to the paper and will not come off easily. (It is advisable to mark the untreated side of the paper to ensure that marbling is done to the treated side.)

As shown in illustration no. 40, the treated paper should then be stacked between large sheets of thick paper, the treated sides together, and large boards on top of and beneath the stack. A weight should then be placed on top of this to increase the pressure on the papers. This prevents wrinkling, and also keeps the sheets from drying out completely, which is desirable to ensure good adhesion of the inks to the paper.

Using ox gall

Ox gall is mixed with the inks to make them spread on the marbling size. The amount of ox gall used with any particular colour of ink depends on when the colour will be used in the pattern to be created. For example, in

(39)   (40)

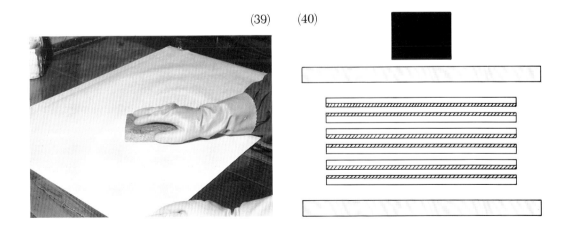

a pattern incorporating five inks, the first colour would probably contain 5 drops of ox gall, the second 10, the third 15, the fourth 20 and the fifth 25. The later the ink is to be used in a pattern, the more ox gall it will need to aid its spread across the size. Since each ink reacts slightly differently to the gall, the amounts will vary, but experience will determine this for you. Ox gall is best kept in a tightly sealed container, and stored in a cool, dark place.

Marbling

Before beginning marbling, use cleaning paper to remove any impurities from the surface of the size. All the colours to be used should be close to hand in the order that they will be required. Brushes should be ready in each bowl or glass that contains the ink.

Transferring marble to paper

Hold the paper, treated side down, at diagonally opposite corners between forefingers and thumbs. Place the lower corner of the paper into the trough and carefully lay the entire length of the paper on to the size without letting it shift (*illustration nos. 41–43*). It is important to avoid trapping air between the paper and the size, as this will result in areas of unmarbled paper.

Remove the paper from the size by drawing it towards you over the rim of the two troughs (if you are using a photographic developing tray), using the rim as a scraper to remove excess size. As soon as possible, place the paper, marbled side up, on a rinsing board and remove the excess size by washing it under a soft flow of water (*illustration no. 44*). The paper is then dried on a drying rack or line.

Collecting data

The design and colours of marbled paper are greatly influenced by small changes in the temperature and humidity of the air, the density of the marbling solution, the varieties of inks used, paper quality, speed of work and timing. If you intend to reuse a pattern quite often, it is advisable to keep a record of all the prevailing circumstances surrounding that pattern's creation in order to return to those same conditions whenever the pattern is to be remade.

Oil marbling

Oil-based colours produce much more vibrant patterns than water-based ones. Carragheen size cannot be used for marbling using oil-based inks/colours. Instead, a size made from gelatin, gum tragacanth or wall paper paste

(41) (42)

(43) (44)

should be employed, and the inks thinned with turpentine or petroleum. The paper does not need to be treated before use, and any colour or size remaining on the surface after marbling should be removed with wet towels. These colours should have marbling brushes and equipment which is kept exclusively for their use.

1 *Turkish marble*

Stone Marble
Agate Marble
Marbre Caillouté Simple
Türkisch Marmor
Stein Marmor
Achat Marmor

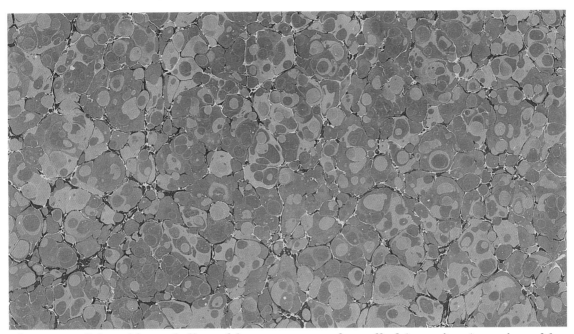

This, one of the oldest of all marble patterns, is also called 'stone' or 'agate' marble, and dates back to the middle of the 15th century. It also forms the base for many other types of marbling.

Three to five colours are generally used to produce this type of marbling. The pictures below show the technique for making a Turkish marble pattern with three colours. First, one colour is thrown on to the surface of the size using a marbling brush (1), after which the two other colours are similarly applied (2, 3).

(1)   (2)   (3)

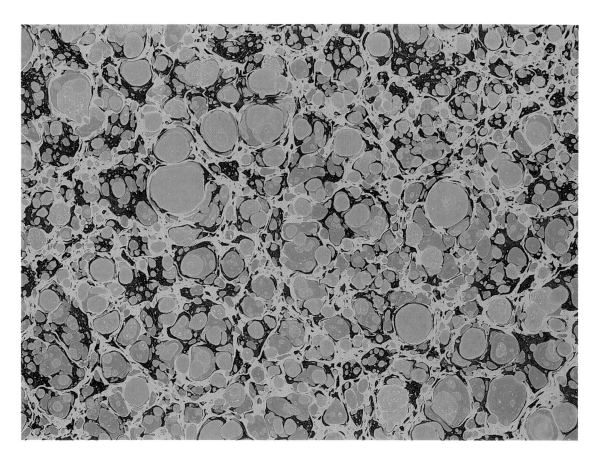

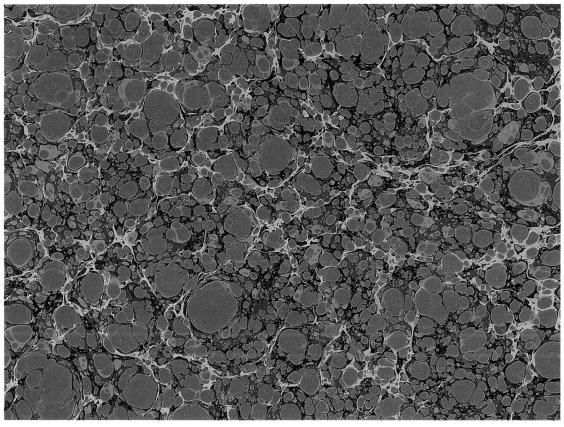

49

2 *Drag marble*

Extra Marble
Marbre Allongé
Marbre Tiré
Schleppmuster Marmor
Zugmuster Marmor

This marble is made in a similar manner to Turkish marble, but after the colours have been applied, the paper is pulled forward while it lies on the size. This elongates the pattern, the primary characteristic of this marble. Drag marble, also called 'extra marble', originated in the 19th century and is similar in style to British marble, gold vein marble and drag Spanish marble.

50

3 *British marble*

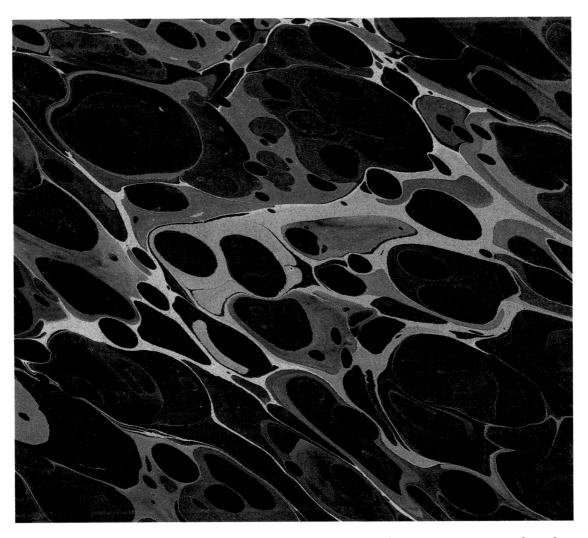

Originating in England at the end of the 19th century, this pattern is created in the same fashion as drag marble. However, in British marble, there is a predominance of grey, black and dark blue, colours not usually associated with drag marble.

4 *Italian marble*

Vein Marble
Hair Vein Marble

Marbre Veiné
Marbre Moucheté

Haarader Marmor
Ader Marmor

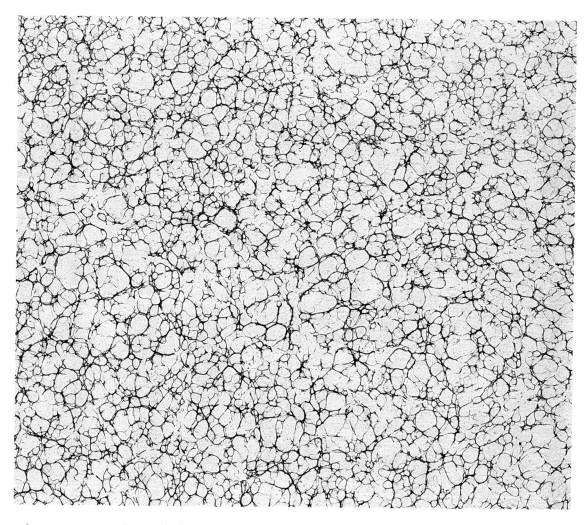

This pattern – also called 'vein marble' or 'hair vein marble' – was created in Italy at the end of the 18th century. Once three colours have been thrown on to the size, a heavy brush is dipped into a strong mixture of soap, spirits and ox gall and moved over a very fine wire mesh so that tiny particles of this mixture mingle with the thrown inks.

5 *Scrotel marble*

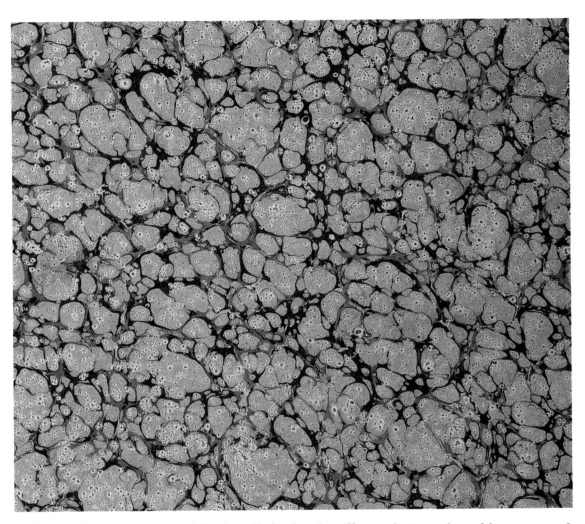

Schrot is the German word for 'small shot' or 'small grain'. Scrotel marble originated in Germany at the beginning of the 18th century. It is produced from two to four colours. A mixture of ox gall and oil is splashed on to the last colour to have been used, producing the characteristic dark spots associated with this type of marble.

6 *Shell marble*

French Shell Marble
Marbre Caillouté Agate
Ringader Marmor
Vogelaugen Marmor

Also called 'French shell marble', this pattern was first created in France at the end of the 18th century. It is created from two to three colours, one of the three colours being mixed with oil. This produces a white outline around some colours and makes them darker towards their centres.

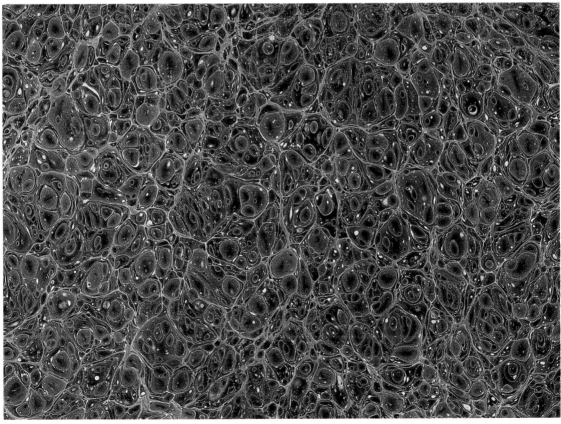

7 *Stormont marble*

'Stormont' is the name of a district in Belfast, Northern Ireland. It is said that this pattern was first used in Dublin in 1750, but did not become popular until the 19th century.

Starting from the basis of a Turkish marble (*see* no. 1), ink mixed with turpentine is thrown on to the trough. This causes the design to appear as if constructed of tiny air bubbles – the primary characteristic of this marble.

8 *Gravel marble*

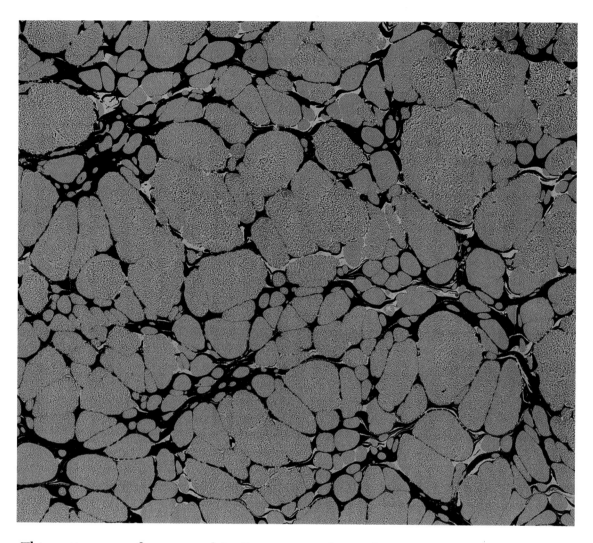

This pattern was first created in Germany in the 18th century. A dark background is created by throwing black ink on to the size, which is followed by lighter colours mixed with ox gall, tartaric acid, wax and caustic soda to produce a rich, luxuriant marble.

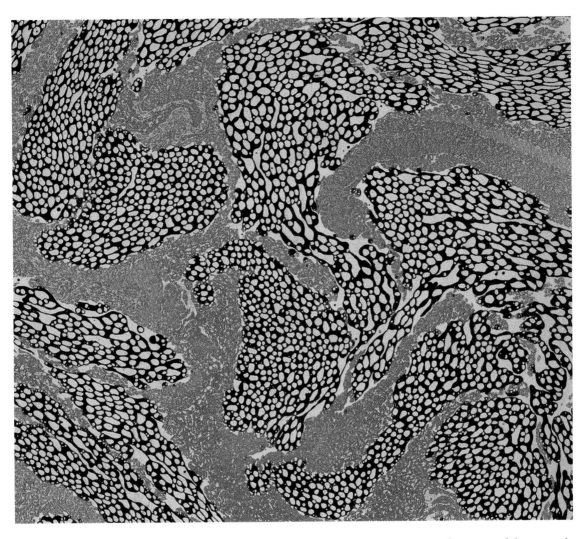

This pattern originated at the beginning of the 20th century and is possibly an oil
marble. It was probably created by throwing a colour on to the trough, to which a
second was added that contains a high percentage of an oily solution. The colours
appear to be left floating a while to be able to react, before the pattern is transferred
on to the paper.

10 *Splinter marble*

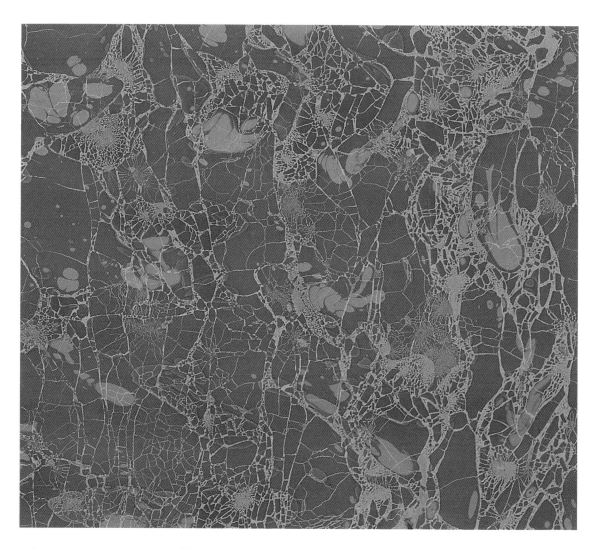

This pattern was created by the turn of the century. The 'skin' on the surface of the size appears to be splintered or cracked. Though we have not been able to reproduce this pattern, we were told that it can be done by using an oil based product used for cosmetic skin care.

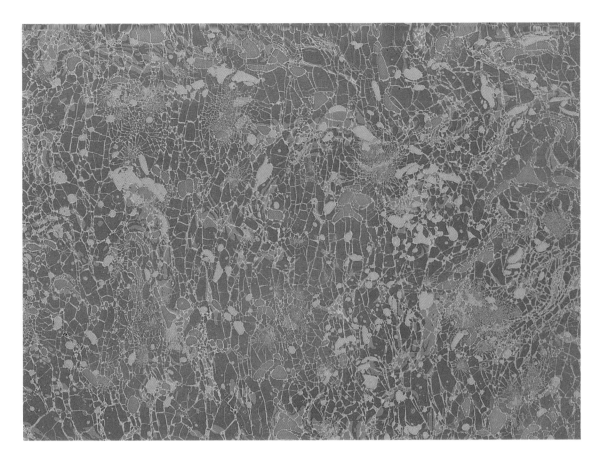

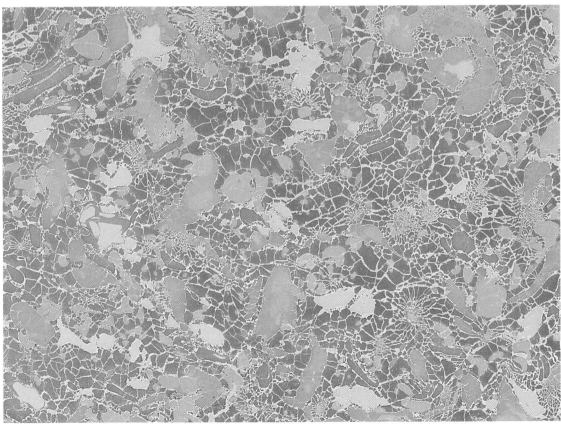

11   *Crystal marble*

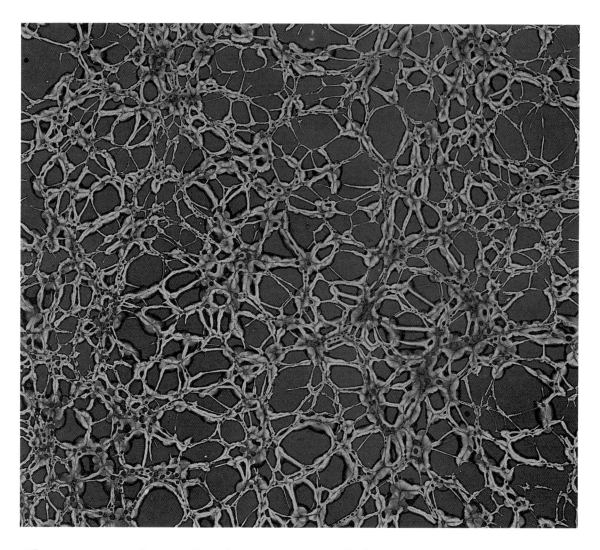

This pattern was first produced in 1970. It is made by splattering ink onto a surface covered with soap spirit or petroleum. I have only been able to create this effect by taking advantage of the chemical reaction which takes place between the products of two different ink makers.

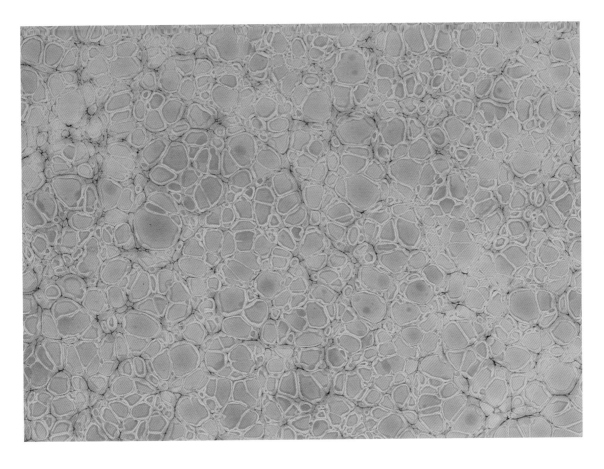

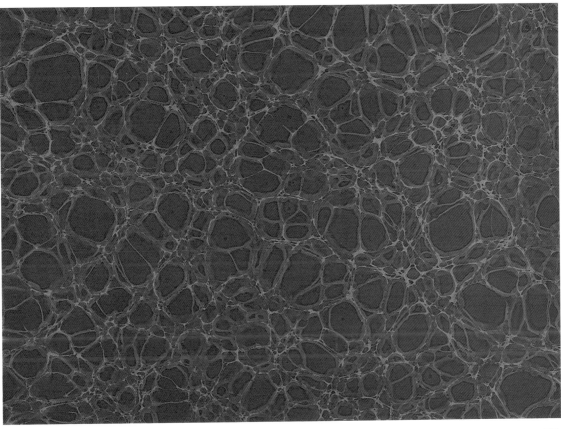

12 *Spanish marble*

Marbre Ombré Droit
Marbre Espagñol
Wellen Marmor
Griechisch Marmor

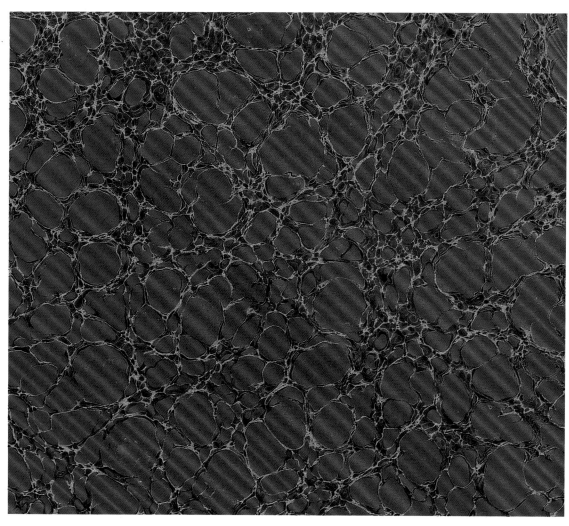

This pattern was first created in Spain at the beginning of the 17th century, and uses a base of Turkish marble (*see* no 1). Once the paper has been laid on to the surface of the size bath, it is agitated to and fro with a regular motion, then the paper is lifted and laid down again repeatedly to produce the linear, wavy pattern which is the chief characteristic of Spanish marble.

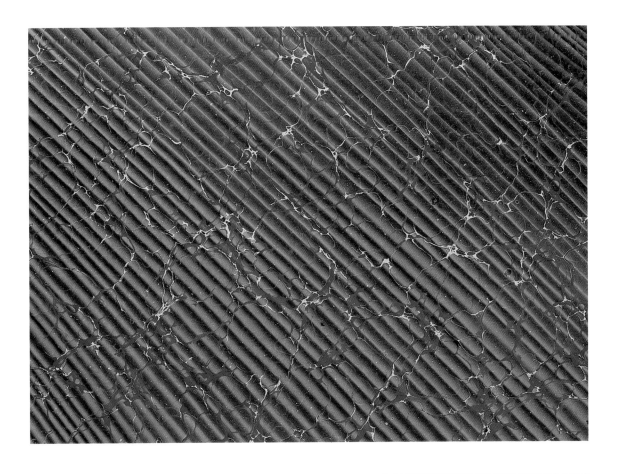

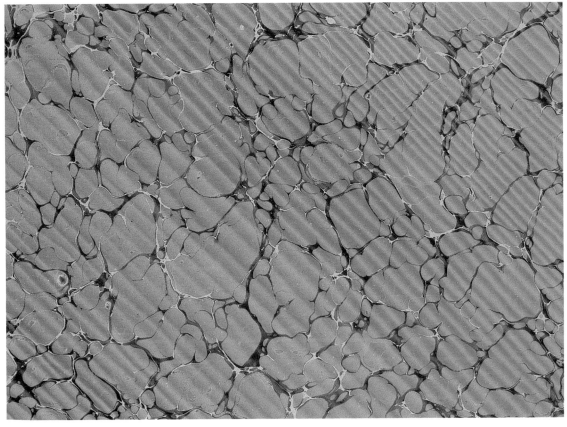

13 *Moiré Spanish marble*

Marbre Ombré Courbe
Marbre Ombré Cassé
Moiré Marmor
Moiré Griechisch Marmor

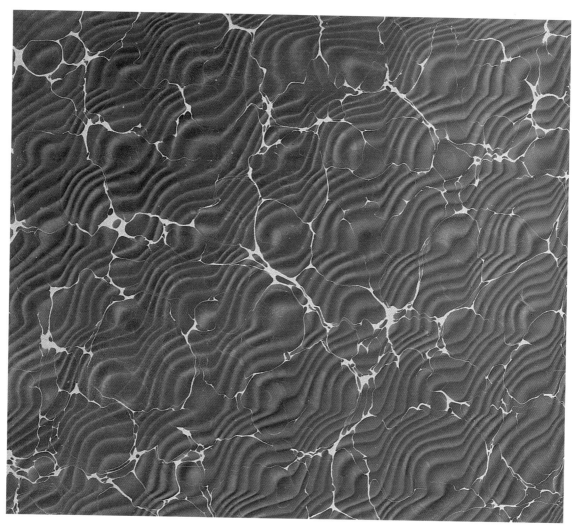

Again, this pattern originates from the beginning of the 17th century. A paper which has first been folded diagonally and vertically is placed on to the surface of a bath containing the Turkish marble base. The paper is then dipped and slightly moved from side to side to create a curved wavy pattern.

Robert Browning, *Poems of Robert Browning*, London, 1912.

14 *Fancy Spanish marble*

Lace Spanish Marble
Marbre Dentelle Espagñol
Spanisch Spitzen Marmor

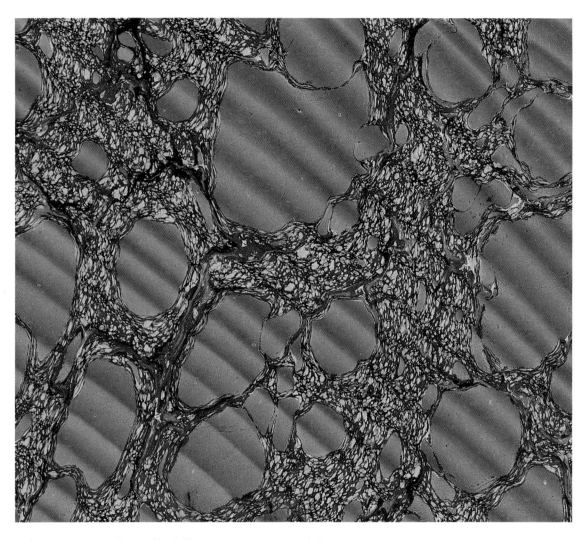

This pattern, also called 'lace Spanish marble', was first created at the beginning of the 17th century. Two or three colours mixed with soap-spirit are thrown on to the size. Then another colour, mixed with ox gall, is added, with the effect of compressing the first colours into a net design. The paper is then treated as for Spanish marble (*see* no. 12) to create a background pattern of wavy lines.

15 *Fantasy marble*

Fancy Marble
Marbre Maître-Relieur
Marbre Fantaisie
Phantasie Marmor

Also called 'fancy marble', this paper was popular from the end of the 19th century to the beginning of the 20th century. Again, the pattern is established from the basis of Turkish marble, but using a very thin size, or even pure water. A stylus of some kind is then employed to manoeuvre the inks into the desired position.

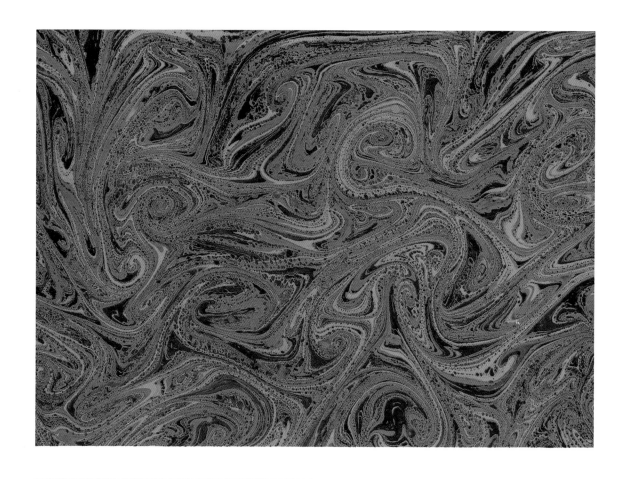

70

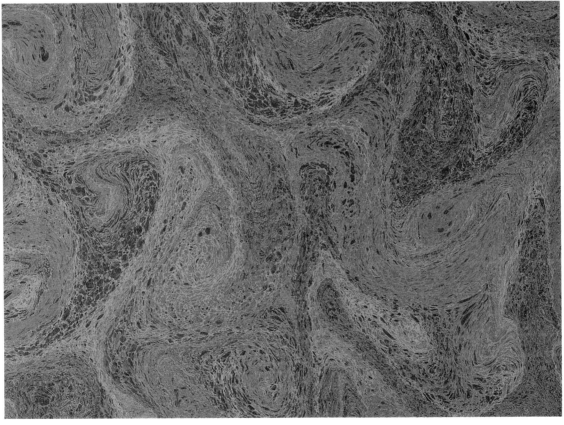

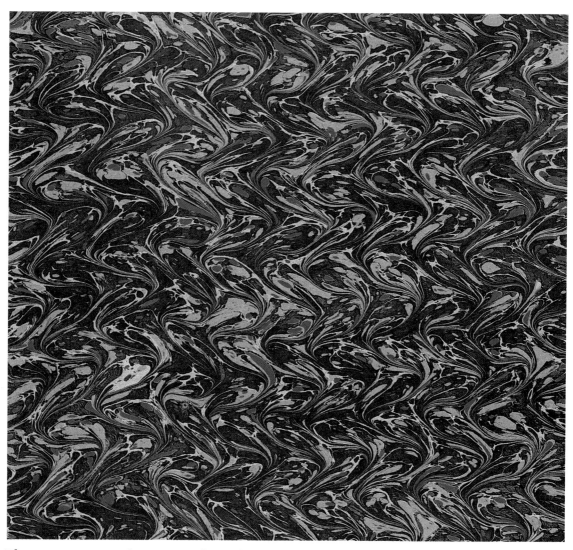

This pattern was first created at the end of the 19th century. It uses a Turkish marble base and is created with the use of a comb with teeth set at 20–80 mm intervals. This is then moved from side to side through the trough, and a print taken from the results.

(1)　　　　　　　(2)　　　　　　　(3)

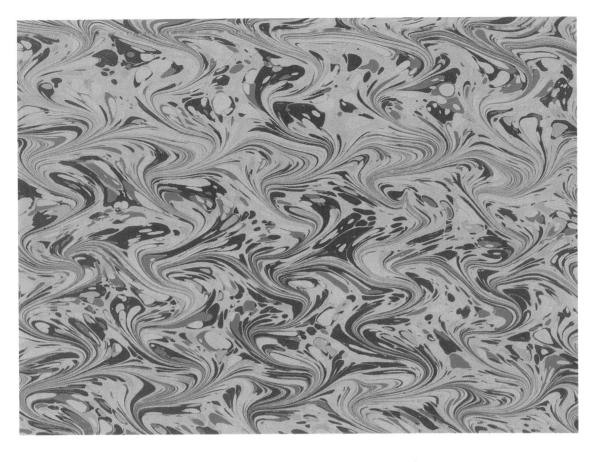

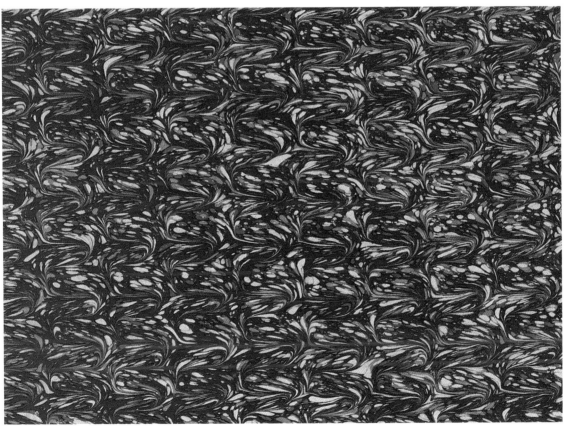

73

17 *Moiré Spanish on modern wave marble*

Ombré Courbe sur Marbre Ondulé Moderne
Moiré auf Modernem Wellen Marmor

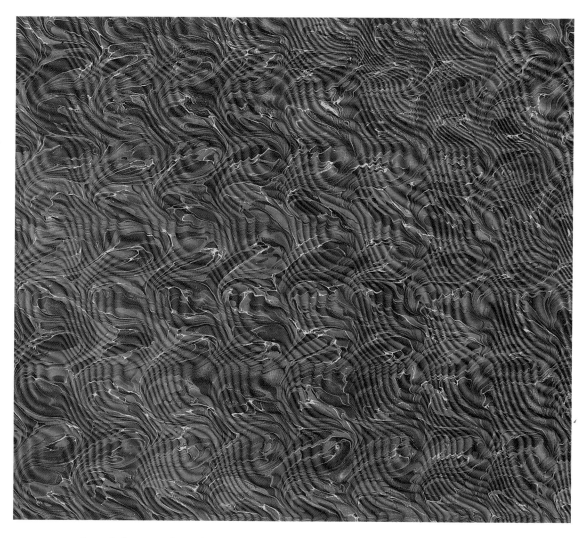

An example of the results of combining several different techniques.

18 *Snail marble*

French Curl Marble
Curl Marble

Marbre Escargot
Marbre Tourniquet
Marbre Coquille
Schnecken Marmor

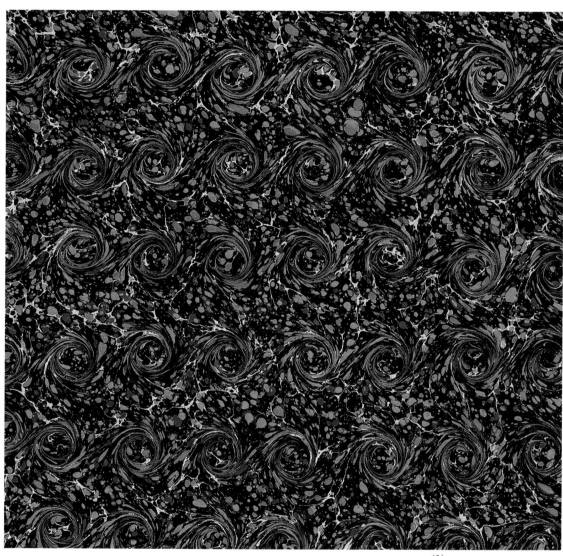

Also called 'curl marble' or 'French curl marble', this pattern was first created in France in about 1660. It was widely used in Europe for the covers and end papers of books until the end of the 19th century. The curls are made with a comb or a stylus (*see diagram*).

(1)

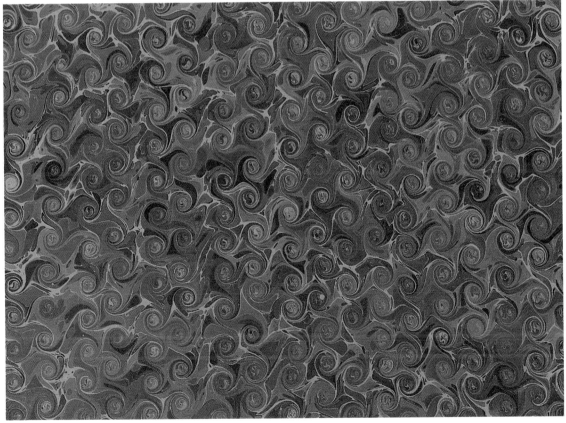

19 *Börjeson marble*

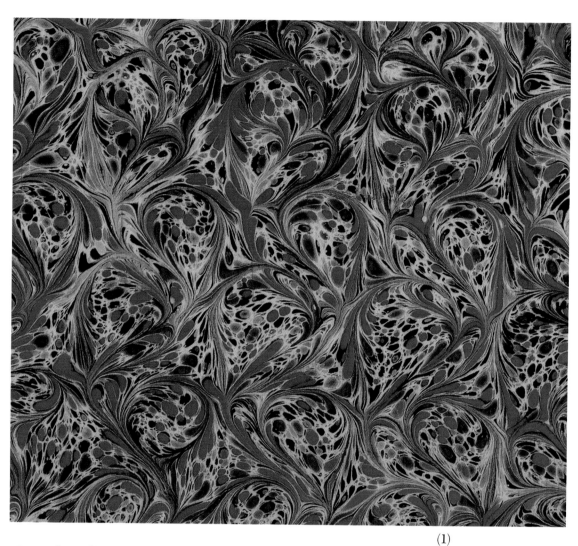

A comb is drawn through a base of Turkish marble, making small circles as it goes (*see diagram*). Both this and the next pattern, created during the 20th century, are named after their inventors, Rolph and Ingeborg Börjeson of Denmark (later Sweden).

(1)

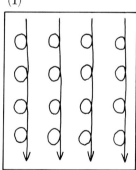

Marbre Goutte sur Börjeson
Tropfen auf Börjeson Marmor

This pattern is created by throwing one or more colours on to a size which has already been prepared with marble as in no. 19.

21 *Sun marble*

Sun Spot Marble
Marbre Soleil
Marbre Oeil de Chat
Marbre Oeil de Tigre
Sonnen Marmor
Tigeraugen Marmor

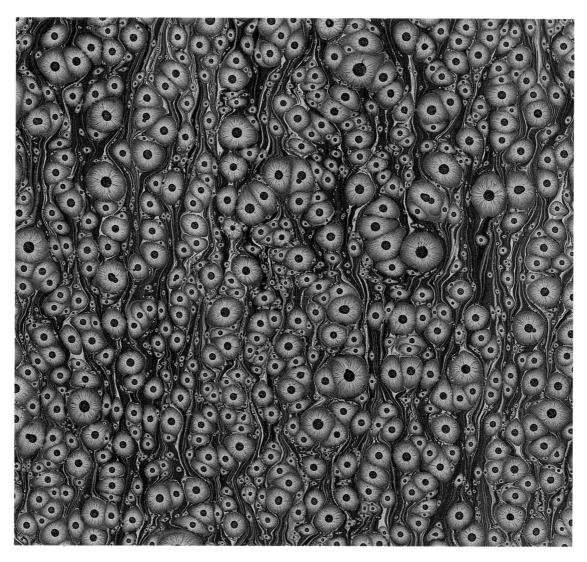

This pattern, also called 'sun spot marble', was first created around 1855. It is made by throwing two or three colours on to the size, through which a comb (with teeth 4–15 mm apart) is then drawn. Finally black ink mixed with 'kreolin' (a commercial product, creosote based, used for wood preservation), lime water and potash solution is thrown on to the pattern. The reaction between the chemical solution and the inks causes sun-like shapes in the pattern.

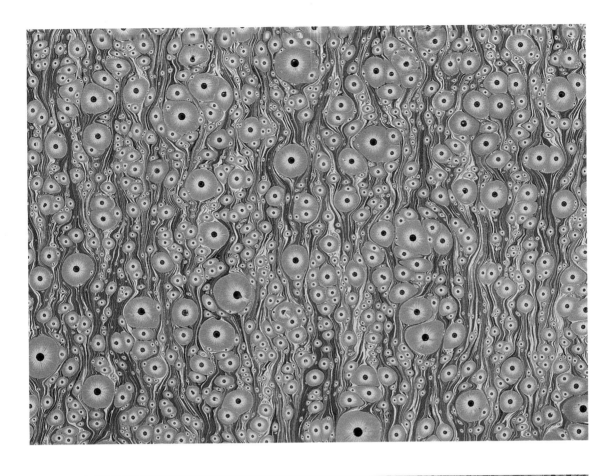

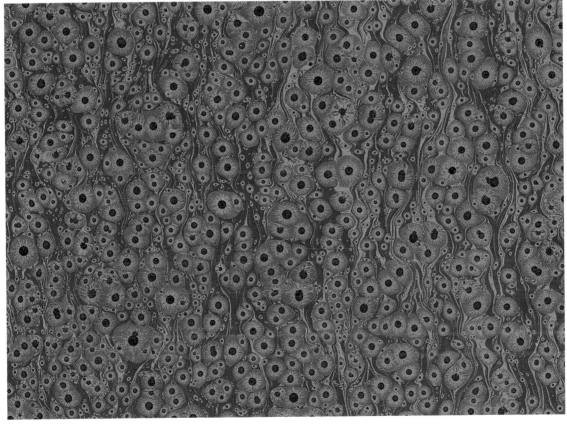

22 *Snail on sun marble*

Marbre Soleil avec Coquille
Schnecke auf Sonnen Marmor

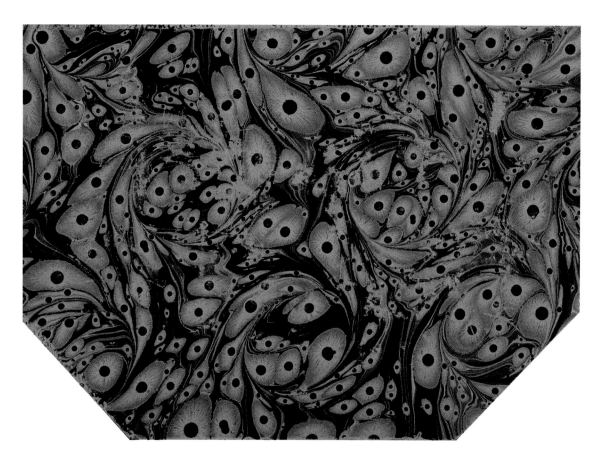

After a sun marble has been created, a comb is used to draw swirls on to the surface of the size.

23 *Zebra marble*

Marbro Zòbro
Gezogener Achat Marmor

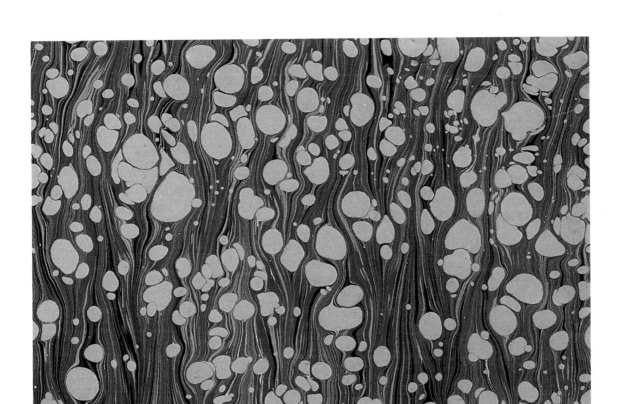

This pattern was popular during the last half of the 19th century. From a Turkish marble base, a comb with teeth set at intervals of 4–15 mm is drawn through the surface, first in a downward direction (1), and then upward (2). One to three additional colours are then splashed on to the surface with a marbling brush (3).

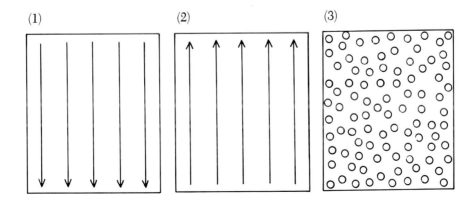

83

24 *Dahlia marble*

Marbre Dahlia
Dahlia Marmor

William Stubbs, *The Constitutional History of England*, 3 vols, Oxford, 1880.

This pattern was first created at the end of the 19th century. It is created from a Zebra marble base (*see* no. 23), on to which another colour, rich with ox gall, is splashed. A second colour is then swirled on to the base through a sieve, and finally a third is lightly sprinkled on top, creating a flower-like pattern.

25 *Antique spot marble*

E. A. Freeman, *The History of the Norman Conquest of England*, 6 vols, Oxford, 1877.

This pattern was popular during the late 18th and early 19th centuries. Small amounts of white ink or pure soap spirits are splashed on to a base of Turkish marble to make this pattern. This effect can also be achieved with zebra marble (*see* no. 23), snail marble (no. 26) and moiré Spanish marble (no. 27).

26 *Antique spot on snail marble*

Antique Spot on French Curl Marble
Antique Spot on Curl Marble

Goutte Antique sur Marbre Escargot
Goutte Antique sur Marbre Tourniquet
Goutte Antique sur Marbre Coquille

Antik auf Schnecken Marmor

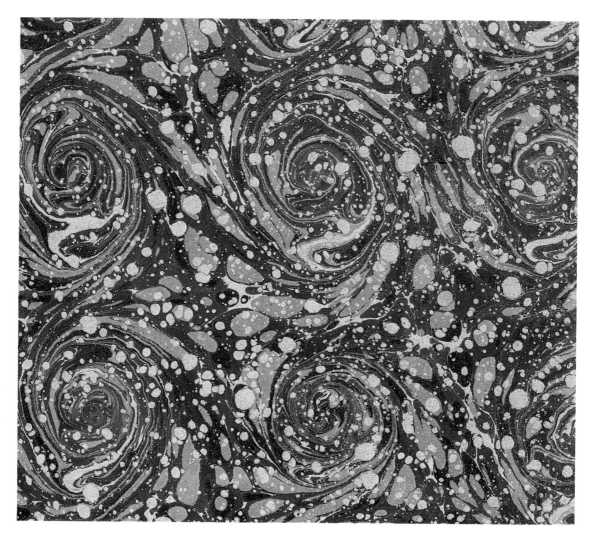

This marble, also called 'antique spot on curl marble' and 'antique spot on French curl marble', is made in a similar manner to a snail marble (*see* no 18). Two to five colours are thrown on to the surface using a brush, then swirls are drawn in the pattern using a comb with teeth set at 50–100 mm intervals. Pale inks or soap spirit are then sprinkled on to the pattern with a marbling brush to make fine, white spots.

27 *Moiré Spanish on antique spot marble*

Ombré Courbe sur Marbre Goutte Antique
Antik auf Moiré Marmor

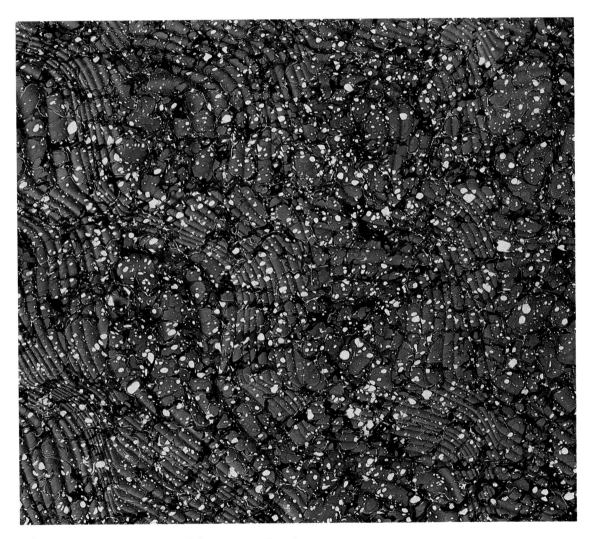

After an antique spot marble pattern has been produced (*see* no 25), the pre-folded paper is placed on the surface of the size and lifted repeatedly, moving it slightly each time to create a curved wavy pattern.

28 *Gloster marble*

Partridge's Eye Marble
Marbre Oeil de Perdrix
Stein Marmor mit Grießtropfen

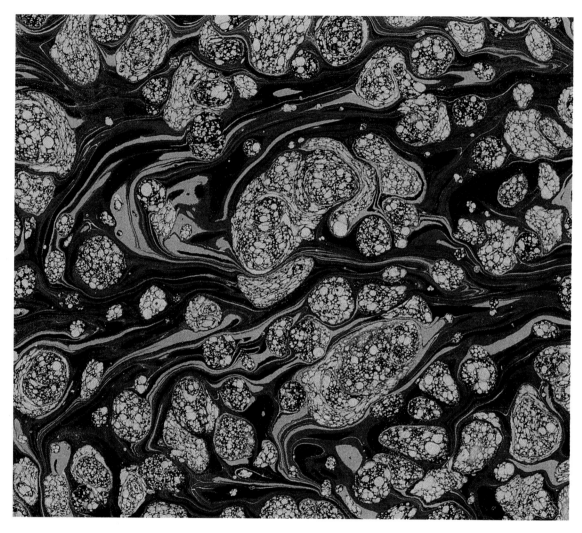

The name 'Gloster' derives from Gloucester in south-west England. This pattern is also called 'partridge's eye marble' and was popular during the second half of the 19th century. After two or three inks are thrown on to the surface in sequence, a comb with teeth set at 4–15 mm intervals is used to make a flowing pattern. Ink mixed with turpentine or soap spirits is then sprinkled on to this to cause small bubble-like spots to appear in the pattern.

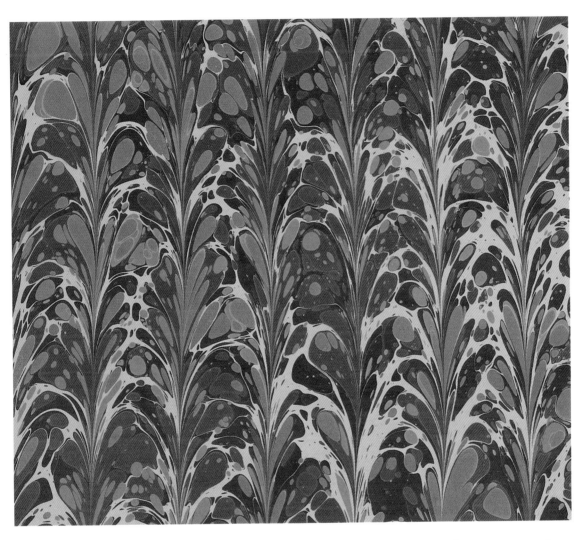

This is called 'fountain marble' because of its resemblance to gushing water. After a Turkish marble pattern has been produced, a comb with teeth set at intervals of 15–25 mm is moved back and forth across the surface of the size to create the pattern.

30 *Wave-combed fountain marble*

Marbre Peigné Ondule Fontaine
Welliger Springbrunnen Marmor

This pattern is created by moving a comb back and forth through a size containing Turkish marble. The comb is moved side to side slightly while being drawn back to create the curves or waves.

31 *Arch marble*

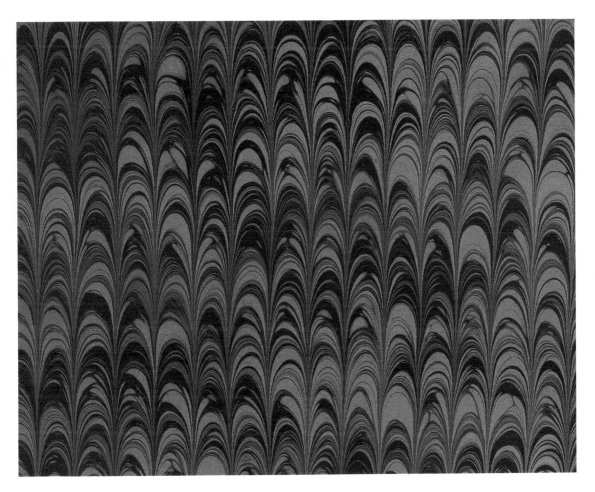

After a Turkish marble pattern has been created, a comb with teeth set at intervals of 4–15 mm is moved across the size from left to right (1), then shifted slightly and moved from right to left (2). To complete the pattern, another comb with teeth set at 15–25 mm intervals is drawn vertically through the trough (3).

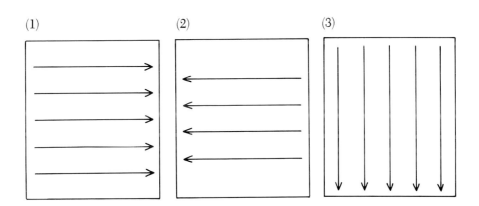

32 *Nonpareil marble*

H. Taine, *Histoire de la Littérature Anglaise*, 4 vols, Paris, 1877.

'Nonpareil' means 'matchless' or 'unrivalled'. This pattern is seen in 17th-century Indian literature, and was used widely in Europe for the sides and endpapers of books printed in the mid–19th century.

Illustration A. To achieve this pattern, two to five colours are dropped sequentially on to the size with a drop brush or eye dropper. A comb with teeth set at intervals of 15–30 mm is inserted on the left side of the marbling trough and moved across its surface to the right (1), then shifted slightly and moved back to the left (2). (In a variation of this technique, the comb can be moved in a wave-like motion.) Finally, a comb with teeth set at intervals of 2–3 mm is inserted at the back of the marbling trough and moved across the size to the front (3).

Illustration B. After the procedures outlined for illustration A have been carried out, the technique requires one more combing from the back of the trough to the front. The last comb used has teeth set at intervals of 8–10 mm.

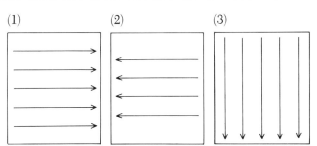

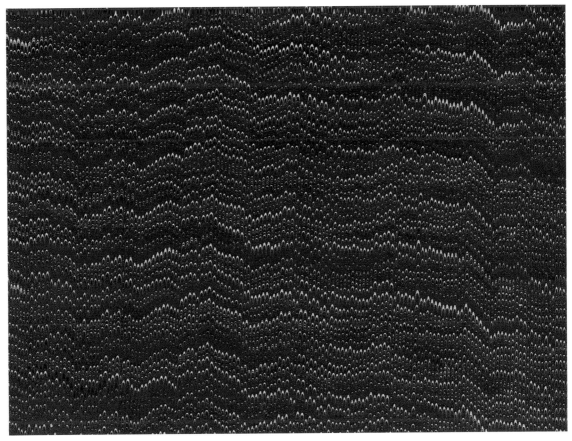

A

B

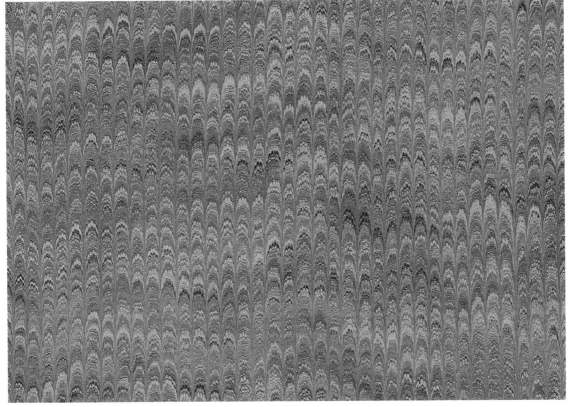

33 *Old Dutch marble*

Henry John Todd, *The Works of Edmund Spenser*, London, 1856.

The oldest known example of this pattern is seen on endpapers of a copy of the New Testament printed in Lyons in 1569. Most of these patterns were made between the early 17th and the 19th centuries in Germany, but were exported to England from Holland – hence 'Dutch' marble. As the name implies, the pattern called 'large Dutch marble' is larger than that of standard Dutch marble and was used on larger books; it generally consists of a red base with the addition of yellow, blue and green, and the occasional use of white.

Illustrations A. A marble is made from four or five colours which are dropped sequentially on to the size. A comb with teeth set at intervals of 5–15 mm is then inserted on the left side of the trough and moved straight across the surface to the

94

A

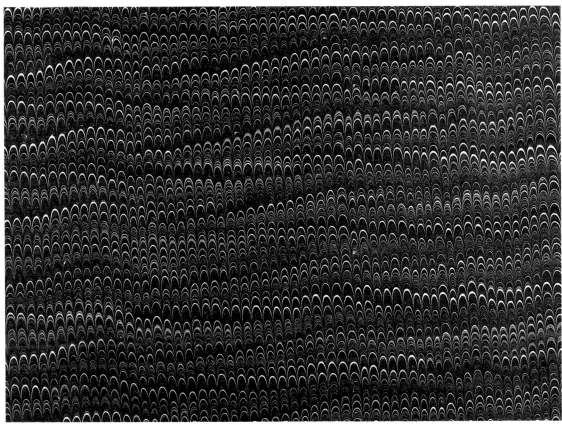

Marius Michel, *La Reliure Française*, Paris, 1880.

right side, then shifted slightly and moved back to the left. Finally, a comb with teeth set at the same intervals is inserted at the back of the marbling trough and moved across the size to the front.

Illustrations B. These are made by following the above procedures, and then a comb with teeth set at 50–150 mm intervals is used to make swirls in the pattern.

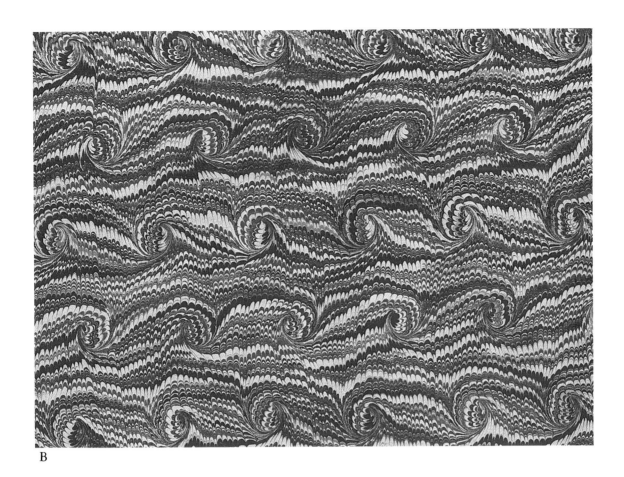

B

34 *Loop marble*

This pattern was first created at the end of the 19th century. It is made by inserting a comb into a trough of two or three colours, and drawing it from left to right and back again. Swirls are then created by pulling the comb from the back to the front of the marbling trough.

35 *Oak leaf marble*

This pattern was popular from the late 19th to the beginning of the 20th century. It is produced using three to five colours and soap-spirit for the white dots. A comb with teeth set at 7–14 mm intervals is then drawn from left to right through the size (1). A second comb with teeth set at 100 mm is then moved in a wave-like motion from the back to the front of the trough (2) and then to the back again with the same motion (3).

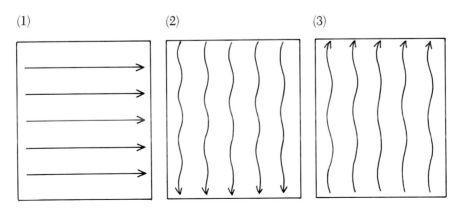

(1)   (2)   (3)

36 *Icarus marble*

Greek mythology tells of Icarus, son of Daedalus, who with his father escaped from the island of Crete by fashioning wings from feathers and wax. Icarus, however, flew so close to the sun that the wax melted, and he fell into the sea and drowned.

This pattern, which calls to mind the beating of Icarus's wings, was first created at the beginning of the 20th century. It is made from a base of arch marble (*see* no. 31) or old Dutch marble (*see* no. 33A), which is then combed as shown in steps 1–4.

(1)   (2)   (3)   (4)

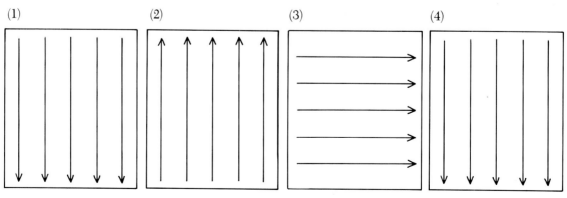

37 *Icarus wave marble*

This marble is made in a similar way to no. 36, but this time the fourth comb is drawn through the size with a wave-like motion.

38 *Wing marble*

Again, this pattern was first created at the beginning of the 20th century. It starts from a base of Icarus marble, through which a comb is drawn from the back to the front of the trough, shifted slightly and then taken back its original starting position.

39 *Ocean wave marble*

Laurence Sterne, *Voyage sentimental en France et en Italie*, Paris, 1884.

From a base of old Dutch marble (no. 33), a comb with teeth set at 100 mm intervals is drawn in a wave-like motion from one side of the trough to the other (1), then shifted up or down and drawn back to the other side (2).

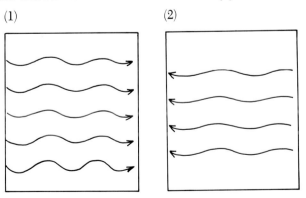

40 *Small wave marble*

H. W. Longfellow, *The Poetical Works of Henry Wadsworth Longfellow*, 2 vols combined, London, 1868.

Once a nonpareil marble has been created (*see* no. 32), a comb with teeth set at intervals or 8–10 mm is inserted at the back of the trough and moved slowly across the surface with a wave-like motion to the front. This pattern was first created in the middle of the 19th century.

(1)

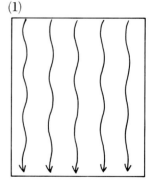

Marbre Peigné Ondulé Large
Groß Gekämmter Wellen Marmor

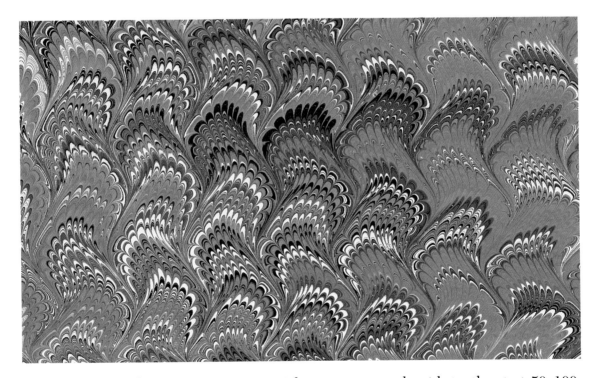

This is made in the same way as no. 40 but using a comb with teeth set at 50–100 mm.

42 *Reverse combed wave marble*

Marbre Peigné Ondulé Retourné
Zurückgezogen Wellig Gekämmter Marmor

After four or five colours have been dropped on to the surface, a comb with teeth set at intervals of 5–15 mm is drawn across the trough from left to right (1). Then it is shifted slightly and returned to the left side (2). (A stylus may be moved through the size in broad wave-like movements as an alternative.) A comb with teeth set at 3–10 mm is then drawn from the front to the back of the trough (3). Finally, a comb with teeth set at 50–100 mm is moved from the back to the front of the tray in a wave-like motion (4).

(1)   (2)   (3)   (4)

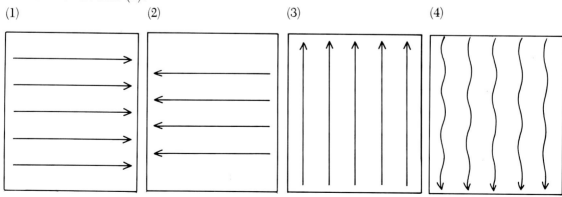

43 *Serpentine marble*

This pattern was first created in the middle of the 19th century. Using a base of two to five colours, a comb with teeth set at 10–30 mm intervals is drawn through the marble as shown in steps 1–4. Finally, a comb with teeth set 14 mm intervals is moved from the back to the front of the size in a wave-like motion (5).

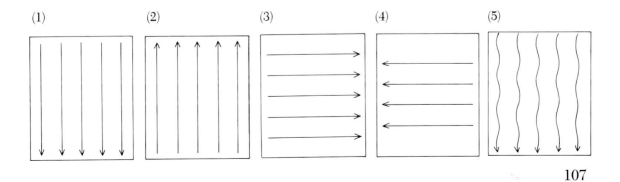

(1)　　　　　　　　(2)　　　　　　　　(3)

(4)　　　　　　　　(5)　　　　　　　　(6)

(7)　　　　　　　　(8)　　　　　　　　(9)

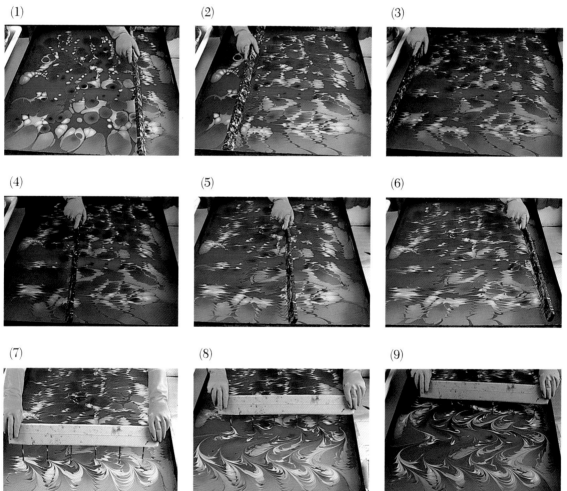

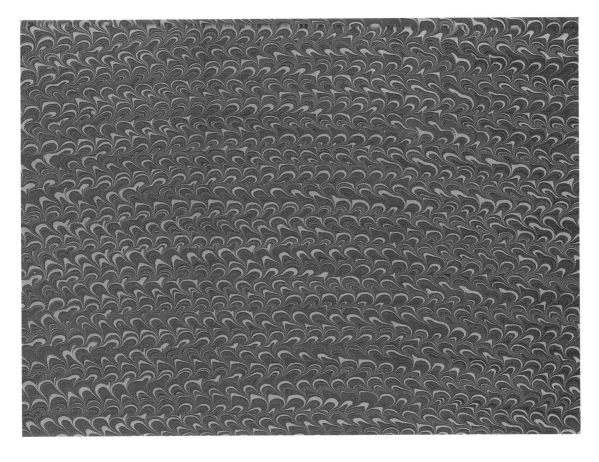

109

44 *Moiré Spanish on serpentine marble*

Ombré Courbe sur Marbre Peigné Serpentin
Moiré auf Gewunden Gekämmter Marmor

After a serpentine marble pattern has been produced (*see* no. 43), the pre-folded paper is placed on the size and lifted repeatedly, moving it slightly each time to create a curved wavy pattern.

45 *Snail on combed marble* Coquilles sur Marbre Peigné
Schnecke auf Kamm Marmor

This pattern was first created during the 19th century. After a nonpareil marble pattern (B) has been made as in no. 32, a comb with teeth set at 50–100 mm intervals is used to make swirls in the pattern.

Examples of combining different marbling techniques.

46 *Feather marble*

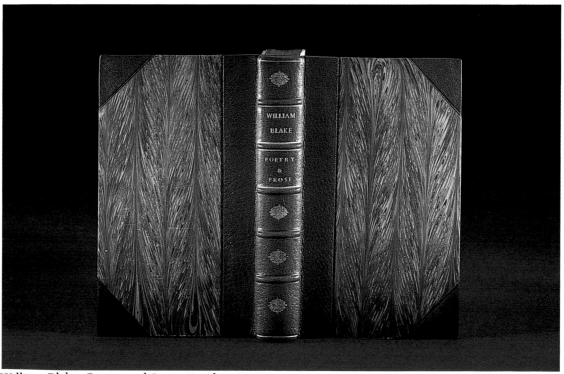

William Blake, *Poetry and Prose*, London, 1927.

This pattern was first created at the beginning of the 17th century, but was most popular from the 19th to the 20th centuries.

Two to five colours are dropped sequentially on to the size, a comb with teeth set at intervals of 10–20 mm is moved from left to right through the size (1) and back to the left again (2). This process is then repeated from the front to the back (3, 4).

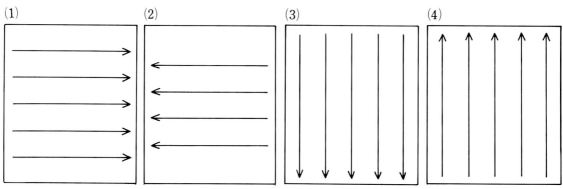

47 Fern marble

Most popular at the beginning of the 19th century, this pattern is produced by using two to five colours, and following the five steps shown.

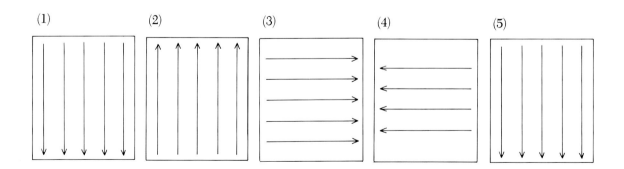

(1) (2) (3) (4) (5)

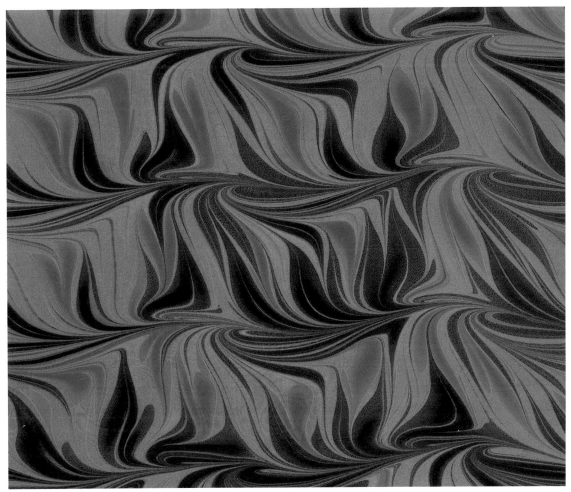

This pattern was first created during the 20th century, and is produced by following the four steps shown. Two to four colours are dropped on to the surface of the size in horizontal rows (1). A comb with teeth set at intervals of 5–10 mm is inserted at the back of the marbling trough and moved straight across the surface to the front (2), then back (3) again. Finally, the comb is inserted on one side and moved across the size to the other side with a 'scribbling' motion (4).

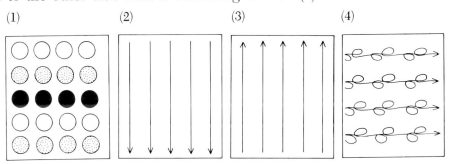

49 *Whirl marble*

(1)

This pattern was first created during the 20th century. Using a base of lotus marble (*see* no. 48), a comb is inserted at the left side of the marbling trough and moved across the surface to the right side with a slight wave-like motion.

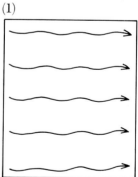

50 *Peacock marble*

Marbre Plume de Paon
Marbre Queue de Paon
Pfauen Marmor
Augen Marmor

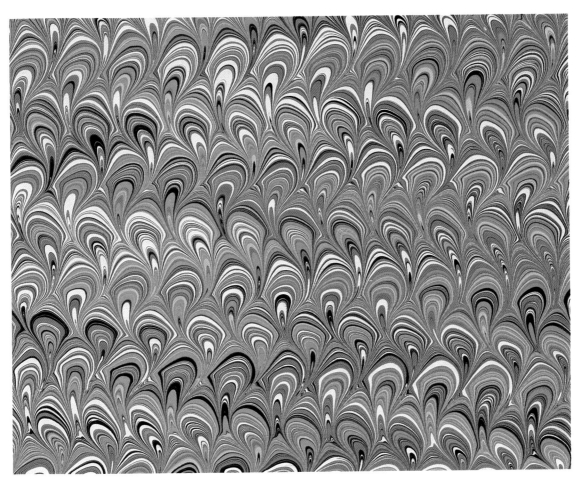

This marble was popular at the end of the 19th century and is produced from a base of two to five colours by following steps 1–5. The fifth combing of the size is done with a comb with two sets of teeth (for a description of this, *see* p. 31).

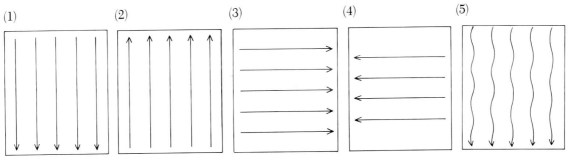

(1) (2) (3) (4) (5)

51 *Bouquet marble*

Marbre Bouquet
Bukett Marmor

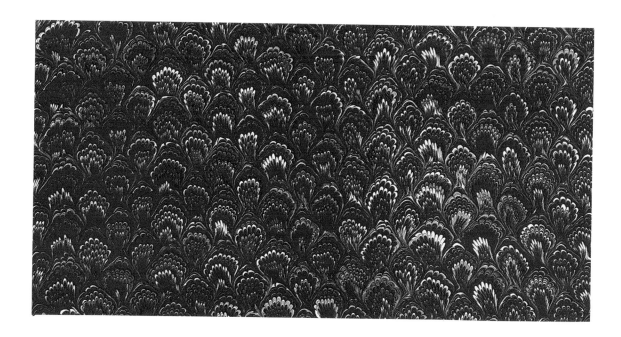

(1)

This pattern was first created at the end of the 19th century. It is made using a nonpareil marble base, and a comb with two sets of teeth which is drawn forward through the size with a wave-like motion.

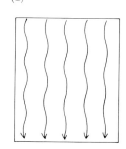

118

52 *Double marble*

Börjeson marble (no. 19) doubled with fountain marble (no. 29).

Zebra marble (no. 23) doubled with nonpareil marble (no. 32).

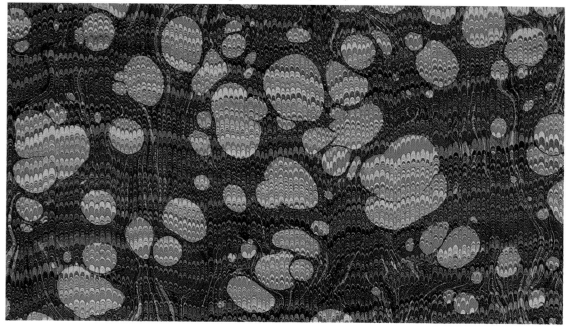

These are papers which are marbled once, treated with alum and then marbled again. Also called 'ghost marble', this pattern was first created in the 17th century.

120

Turkish marble (no. 1) doubled with oak leaf marble (no. 35).

Snail marble (no. 18) doubled with Icarus wave marble (no. 37).

53 *Gold vein marble*

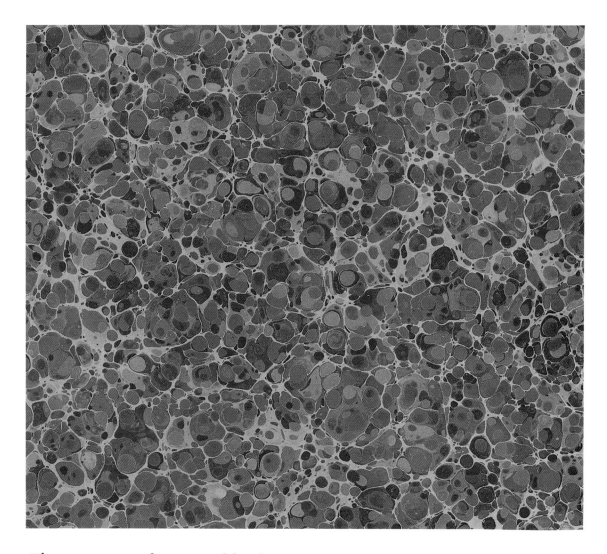

This pattern was first created by the French father and son team, the Le Bretons, in the 17th century. A marbling brush is used to throw bronze inks on to the surface, which forms the basis for a Turkish marble pattern. The resulting pattern has a gold vein running through it.

Charles Kingsley, *The Heroes, or Greek Fairy Tales for My Children*, London, 1930.

54 *Gold vein on drag marble* Veine d'Or sur Marbre Allongé
Goldader auf Schleppmuster Marmor

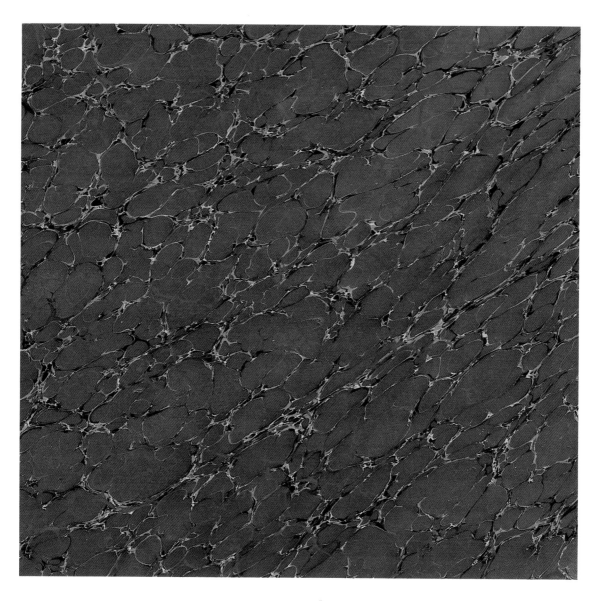

This pattern is formed in the same way as no. 53, and is then dragged across the surface of the size as in no. 2.

William Harrison Ainsworth, *Mervyn Clitheroe*, London, 1858.

55 *Gold vein on moiré Spanish marble*

Veine d'Or sur Marbre Ombré Courbe
Veine d'Or sur Marbre Ombré Cassé
Goldader auf Moiré Marmor
Goldader auf Griechisch Marmor

This pattern was first used in Germany and France in the 19th century. It is made by first creating a moiré Spanish marble (*see* no. 13), and then adding gold veins to the paper using lithographic techniques (*see* no. 53).

126

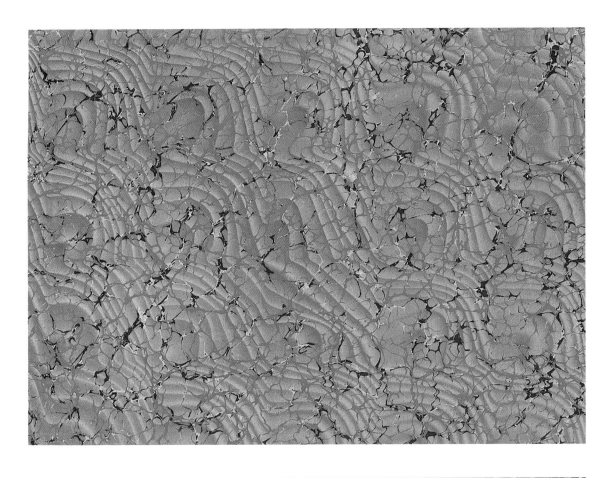

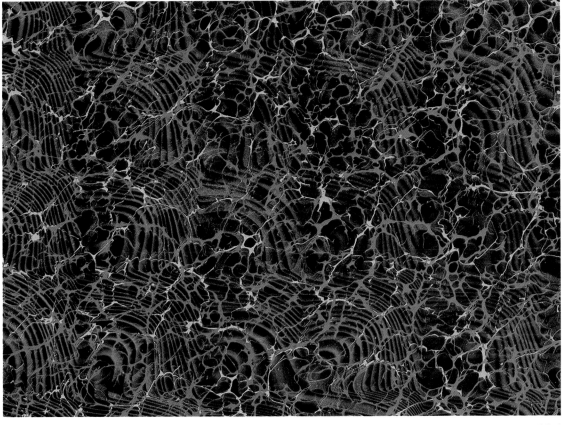

56 *Gold vein on snail marble*

Gold Vein on French Curl Marble
Gold Vein on Curl Marble

Veine d'Or sur Marbre Escargot
Veine d'Or sur Marbre Tourniquet
Veine d'Or sur Marbre Coquille

Goldader auf Schnecken Marmor

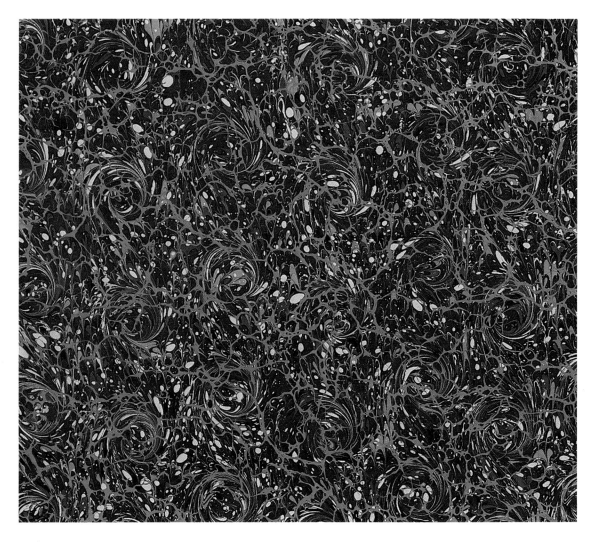

After a snail marble pattern has been made as shown in no. 18, bronze veins are printed on to the marbled paper. This pattern, which is also called 'gold vein on curl marble' or 'gold vein on French curl marble' was first used in Germany and France in the 19th century.

57 *Gold vein on antique spot marble*

Veine d'Or sur Marbre Goutte Antique
Goldader auf Antik Marmor
Goldader auf Schwedisch Marmor

After an antique spot marble pattern has been produced as shown in no. 25, bronze veins are printed on to the marbled paper. This pattern was also first used in Germany and France in the 19th century.

58 *Gold vein on moiré Spanish serpentine marble*

Veine d'Or sur Marbre Ombré Courbe Serpentin
Goldader auf Gewunden Gekämmter Moiré Marmor

After a serpentine marble pattern has been produced as shown in no. 43, the curved wavy pattern of moiré Spanish marble is made on it as shown in no. 13, then bronze veins are printed on to the marbled paper.

These patterns all show the effects of applying gold vein marbling to various techniques.

59 *Moiré Spanish marble paper*

Ombré Courbe Marbre sur Veine d'Or
Moiré auf Goldader Marmor

Thomas Hughes, *Tom Brown's Schooldays*, Oxford, 1907.

From a base of gold vein marble (*see* no. 53), the pre-folded paper is placed on the size and lifted repeatedly, each time moved slightly to create a curved wavy pattern.

Matthew Arnold, *Essays in Criticism*, 2 vols, London, 1910.

Dante Gabriel Rossetti, *The Collected Works of Dante Gabriel Rossetti*, 2 vols, London, 1890.

60 *German marble*

H. Taine, *Histoire de la Littérature Anglaise*, 4 vols, Paris, 1877.

This and the following seven patterns (nos. 60–67) make use of methods whereby ink is applied directly to the paper. Because of this, they cannot be strictly termed marbled papers.

The pattern known as 'German marble' was created in the mid–19th century. After a base colour has been laid, marbling brushes are used to sprinkle coloured inks directly on to the surface of the paper in fine spots.

61 *Flame marble*

Papier Flambé
Flammen Marmor

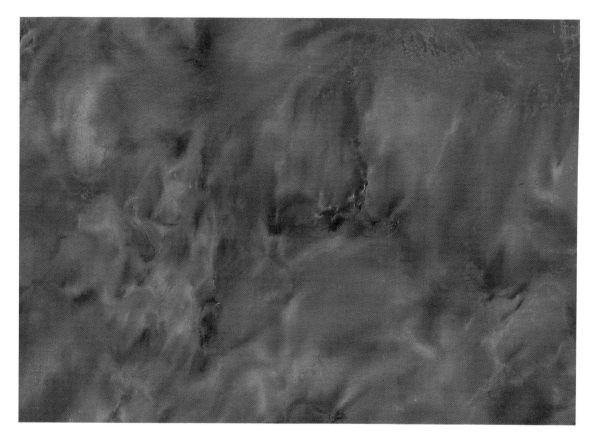

This pattern was created by the Frenchman Edmond Koch in 1920. Ink is dropped on to a very smooth surface such as a lithographic stone, polished marble or glass. Bronzed colours are then sprayed over this. The resulting pattern is lifted on to a piece of paper.

136

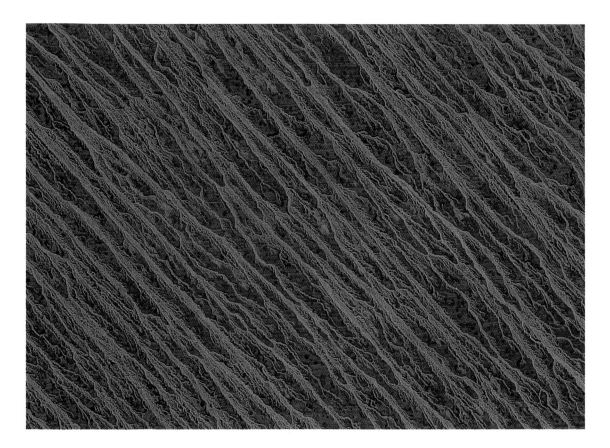

A hand mop (1) is used to apply thin, coloured paste to the paper (2). Then diluted paste of another colour is sprinkled on to this, using a marbling brush (3). The paper is affixed to a board (4) and tilted at an angle of 20–45 degrees to allow the watery paste colours to run, forming the pattern.

(1)   (2)   (3)   (4)

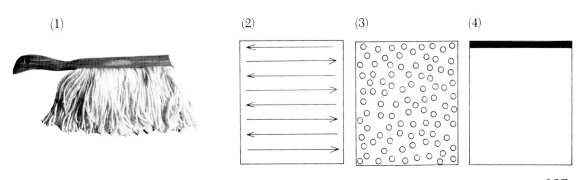

63 *Crater marble*

Marbre Cratère
Krater Marmor

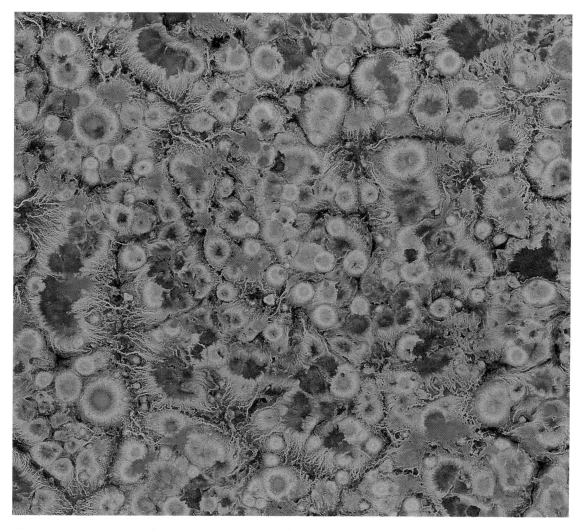

This paper was popular in France around the turn of the century. Three or four colours are put into separate pump-action spray guns. The nozzles of the guns are held close against the paper and the ink 'jetted' out, producing a succession of crater-like images separated by dark canals. The pattern is controlled entirely by its creator.

64 *Root marble*

This pattern was first created at the end of the 19th century. One colour is applied to the paper as a base. Ink is dropped from a marbling brush on to this while it is still wet. The wet paper, supported by a board, is then lifted and held at different angles to let the inks run freely. Soap spirit may be added to the paper to aid the process.

65 *Morris marble*

Robert Browning, *The Poetical Works*, 2 vols combined, London, 1899.

This pattern was created at the end of the 19th century, possibly by E. W. Morris, a London printer, or by another individual named Morris who worked in Oxford. A sponge is used to soak the paper with water. Colours are then dropped on to the paper, which are allowed to run into each other creating a watercolour effect. The paper can be moved slightly to allow the colours to move more freely. Both water- and oil-based colours may be used for this process, each producing a different effect.

141

66 *Spot marble*

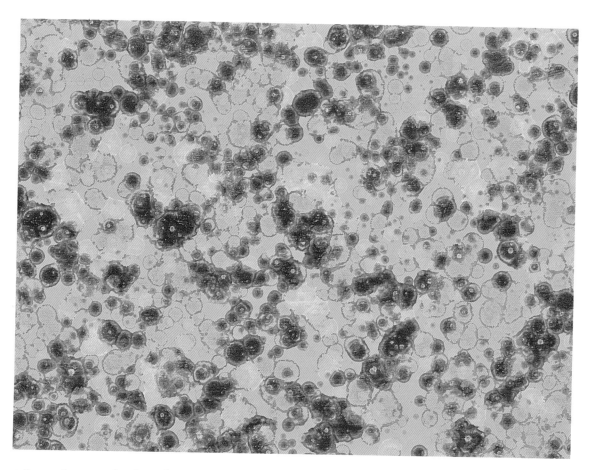

After ink is applied to the paper with a sponge to provide a background colour, two or three other colours are dropped directly on to the paper. The base colour is responsible for the effect created.

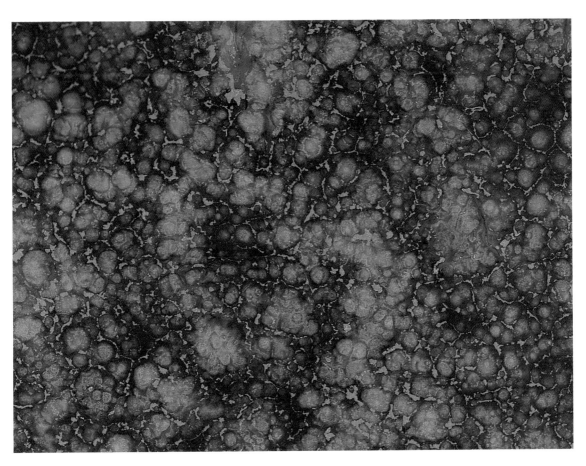

Bronze ink is used as the background colour to this pattern, which is made in the same way as spot marble (*see* no. 66). Colours and silver ink are dropped on to the paper, the bronze base forcing them to contract and produce this striking effect.

BIBLIOGRAPHY

Adam, Paul, *Das Marmorieren des Buchbinders auf Schleimgrund und im Kleister-verfahren* . . . Düsseldorf, Halle, a. S.: W. Knapp, 1906.

Adams, Charles M., 'Some Notes on the Art of Marbling Paper in the Seventeenth Century,' *Bulletin of the New York Public Library*, Vol. 51, No. 7, July 1947.

Doizy, Marie-Ange, and Stephane Ipert, *Le Papier Marbré*, Paris: Éditions Techno-rama, 1985.

Easton, Phoebe J., *Marbling: A History and a Bibliography*, Los Angeles: Dawson's Book Shop, 1983.

Fichtenberg, M., *Nouveau Manuel Complet du Fabricant de Papiers de Fantaisie*, Paris: Roret, 1852.

Franke, A., *Die Buchbinderei*, Leipzig: Verlag Bernh. Friedr. Voigt, 1922.

Haemmerle, Albert, *Buntpapier: Herkommen, Geschichte, Techniken, Beziehungen zur Kunst*, Munich: Georg D. W. Callwey, 1961.

Halfer, Josef, *Die Fortschritte der Marmorierkunst*, Budapest, 1885. (*The Progress of the Marbling Art* . . ., translated by Herman Dieck, Buffalo, N. Y., 1894.)

Kersten, Paul, *Anleitung zur Herstellung von Buntpapieren für den Eigenen Gebrauch*, Stuttgart, 1930.

Kersten, Paul, *Die Marmorierkunst*, Halle, Germany, 1922.

Loring, Rosamond B., *Decorated Book Papers*, Cambridge, Mass.: Dept. of Graphic Arts, Harvard College Library, 1952.

Middleton, Bernard, C., *A History of English Craft Bookbinding Technique*, London: Hafner Publishing Co., 1963.

Petræus, B., *Marmoreringsprocessens Principer*, Stockholm: Sveriges Bokbinderi- och Pappers-emballageförening, 1949.

Sinclair, Hugh, *The Whole Process of Marbling Paper and Book-Edges*, London, 1820.

Sumner, James, *The Mysterious Marbler*, London: T. J. Dunning, 1854.

Wakeman, Geoffrey, *English Marbled Papers: A Documentary History*, Lough-borough: Plough Press, Great Britain, 1978.

Weichelt, August, *Buntpapier-Fabrikation*, Berlin: Carl Hoffman, 1909.

Weisse, Franz, *Die Kunst des Marmorierens*, Stuttgart: Max Hettler Verlag, 1940.

Winckler, O. Th., *Die Marmorierkunst: Aus der Buchbinder-Werkstatt*, Leipzig, 1880.

Woolnough, Charles W., *The Art of Marbling* . . ., London: A. Heyalin, 1853.

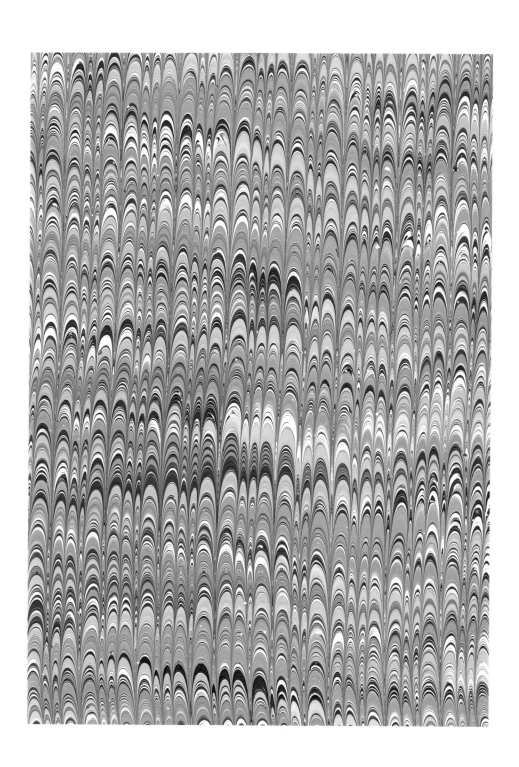

INDEX IN ENGLISH

INDEX EN FRANÇAIS

INDEX IN DEUTSCH

AFTERWORD

I first came across marbled paper in an original work on political science that I found at a second-hand bookstore called Subonso in the Kanda section of Tokyo when I was a college student. The book, which I still have, is a half-leather binding with Spanish marble sides. At that time, I thought that it was pretty, but it did not arouse any further interest.

After I finished college in 1971, I had the chance to study in England for about four and a half years. Since I considered myself a book lover, and I was based in London, I visited many places, including the great British Library, the Victoria & Albert Museum, the Bibliothèque Nationale in Paris, the royal Libraries in Den Haag and Stockholm, where I had the chance to examine a large number of rare books. I also began to become increasingly interested in beautiful books bound with marbled paper, and I wanted to find out how marbled paper was actually made.

I started by visiting such top-class marbled paper producers as Mr Lundberg of Denmark, Ingeborg Börjeson of Sweden and Tini Scharnweber-Bremer (who later became my wife), and I learned how to produce marbled paper directly from them. I also saw collections of precious marbled paper at the New York Public Library, the Metropolitan Museum of Art and elsewhere. At the same time, I began to collect scientific books and articles about marbled paper. I also started to collect precious original marbled paper that had been produced between the 16th to 20th centuries. At present, my collection comprises about 10,000 sheets of 400 patterns. All of the colour examples in this book were selected from this collection.

In this book, I wanted to describe marbled paper in the greatest detail possible, using my collected materials and my experience in the production of marbled paper. During the long time that this took, my wife Tini shared a huge amount of her material and knowledge with me, without which I would have been unable to publish this book. I am confident that this is the first book to have introduced so many marbled patterns at one time.

The section 'The History and Development of Marbled Paper' is an expanded and revised version of an article that I wrote which was published in the February 1983 issue of *Senshoku Alpha*.

I hope this book proves to be of value to those studying design and to book lovers, as well as to those involved with libraries, old books, publishing, printing and bookbinding, and helps them discover the beauty of traditional marbled paper from Europe (which I personally believe originated from Japanese *suminagashi*).

EINEN MIURA
Tokyo, 18 May 1989

CAREER

Einen Miura was born in Japan in 1944. After graduating from Waseda University in Tokyo, he did graduate work at London University. There he married Kerstin Tini Scharnweber-Bremer, one of the best-known designer binders in the world.
In 1976, the Miuras established the first orthodox design–binder studio in Japan. Because of the enormous interest that Tini Miura's exhibitions created, Einen Miura founded the Japan Bibliophile Binding Society, of which he is chairman, to help bring an understanding of Western printing and binding history and techniques to Japanese book lovers. Einen and Tini Miura divide their time between their studios in Tokyo and New York, and recently Mr Miura took a group of Japanese bibliophiles on a library tour throughout the United States where they could admire the special collections that were graciously shown to them.

As well as his lectures which aim at creating a wider market for the next generation of young aspiring bookbinders in Japan, Einen Miura has published three books: K. Sakamoto's *Books about Books* (1980), C. Franklin's *Private Presses* (1983), and his own *Fascinating Marble Paper* (1988), published here as *The Art of Marbled Paper*. He also has written *Classic Marble Papers* (1988). His dedication to books is easily understood through his activities.

SHIRO HAYASHI
Honorary professor, Meikai University
Tokyo, spring 1989